Living in the Light of Eternity

K. P. YOHANNAN

LONGWOOD COMMUNICATIONS

Printed in the United States of America
International Standard Book Number: 0-9632190-6-5
Library of Congress Catalog Card Number: 93-079545

Unless otherwise noted, all Scripture quotations are from the King James Version of the Bible. Personal emphasis (noted by italics) has also been added in various verses.

Published by:
Longwood Communications
1310 Alberta Street
Longwood, FL 32750
407-260-0016

Gospel for Asia
1932 Walnut Plaza
Carrollton, TX 75006
214–416–0340

Dedication

This book is dedicated to the staff of Gospel for Asia all around the world. These brothers and sisters share my vision and burden for the lost of Asia. They have sacrificed so much in order to serve the native missionaries and enable them to win millions to Jesus.

Living in the Light of Eternity

Table of Contents

Acknowledgments

This book is the result of over ten years of traveling and speaking to God's people from all walks of life. What you read in this volume has been used by God to change the lives of many. I am grateful to the Lord for allowing me to have a part in touching these lives for His kingdom's sake.

This project would not have been possible without my secretary Heidi Chupp. With tireless determination, she typed and proofread the manuscript, added words to make things clear, corrected my spelling and grammar and arranged the chapters in logical order. She did all this and much more without one word of complaint.

I also want to thank Debi Carroll for helping to transcribe the majority of these messages from tapes.

Finally, I want to thank my family—my wife, Gisela and my children, Daniel and Sarah—for their love and support, without which it would have been impossible to stay in the battle. They stand with me in our commitment to reach our generation for the Lord.

K.P. Yohannan

Introduction

Recently I found myself in an interesting conversation—with my pen! It was a bit one-sided, perhaps, but I learned some things from that talk.

For as long as I can remember, even in my school days, I have always used a fountain pen. The one I own today is a gift from a friend of mine. It's quite a nice pen, and I enjoy using it.

One day, I sat alone at my desk, writing with my pen. As I sat there, I looked at that pen in my hand and began a conversation. "Pen," I said, "I really like you. I think you're the finest thing there is. I don't even loan you out to anyone else."

"Well, thank you," I imagined the pen to respond. "It's nice to know I am appreciated."

"Pen," I continued, "you are really part of my

9

personality. My signature—who I am—has been shaped by you. There is something about you that no one else can claim. But I'm sad to tell you, Pen, that after a few years go by, you will no longer be mine."

"What do you mean?" my pen asked. "Are you planning to give me away?"

"You know, Pen," I explained, "right now I am forty-two years old. If I added one hundred years to my life, I can't imagine that I would be around anymore. You might be—but I will be gone.

"So, Pen, I'll use you as long as I can. But I'll not hold you so tight that I will have to weep over you when the end comes."

As you begin to read through this book, I challenge you to take a fresh look at how you are investing your life—your time, your energy, your abilities.

You have only one life. It is your choice, whether you realize it or not, how you will invest it. Will you spend it on yourself and your own pleasures, or will you throw yourself at the feet of Jesus and tell Him, "Here I am—send me"?

When you live your life in the light of eternity, the treasures so valued by the world suddenly become worthless. "Things" don't matter any more—and souls become precious.

It is my heart's prayer that as you come to the end of this book, you will not close it and simply say, "Well, that was a challenging book," and then go on with your life the way it was before.

Take some time to pray right now, and ask the Lord to use this book to soften your heart, fill your eyes with tears and move you out of your comfort zone and into a world that is lost and dying without Christ.

I challenge you to go beyond the knowing, the "I've-heard-it-before" mentality. Step into the uncertainty of doing the will of God. It will be the beginning of a serious, honest walk with Jesus. I can assure you, a life spent in this way will be eternally worth it.

May the Lord bless you and speak to you as you read through these pages.

K.P. Yohannan
Carrollton, Texas

Living in the Light of Eternity

PART I

SOMETHING TO LIVE FOR

Chapter 1

LIFT UP YOUR EYES

W hat do you consider to be the basic essentials of life? Let's make some mental notes of the things we need to survive, or just to get by.

We'll start with a house. How many rooms do we need to survive? All right, we have a one-bedroom house. Let's add a tiny bathroom—that should be enough. But what about a kitchen? Perhaps a small one. Refrigerator? Can't live without it! We'll need running water too—at least cold, and maybe we can add hot as well.

What about electricity? We absolutely need that. Carpeting? Well, it does get cold in the winter. What about a TV? We need to know what is going on in the world.

Let's move on now to the car. What kind do we

need? A small, domestic-made car will be the cheapest. We should also consider a motorcycle or bicycle—cheaper still.

How about clothes? Now, we're not talking about what we want but only the *basic essentials*. A few pairs of pants, a couple shirts, some socks and underclothes will do. Shoes? One pair is fine.

Personal care—do we need all those shampoos and conditioners? A piece of soap will do just fine. Let's also include some deodorant. Perhaps we can add a mirror—but let's keep it small.

Our list is far from finished. What happens when we have a headache? We'd better keep some aspirin on hand. Oh, and don't forget the vitamins and bandages.

How about financial security? Well, we need at least a small bank account with a few dollars in it.

We don't want to forget the children. They will also need a few items of clothing and perhaps some toys to keep them busy.

Now let's look over our mental list and think carefully about what we have included. What does it *really* take to live?

In your mind's eye, light a match. Hold it to the list. Watch it burn until all that is left is a wisp of ash.

You don't need *any* of these things—however basic they may be—to live.

There are millions of people in the world who live and die on the streets of New York, Rio, Bombay, Mexico City and elsewhere. They sleep in cardboard huts, under bridges and in cement sewer pipes. And they "get by" without any of the essentials we have written on our list.

Whether we like it or not, we also can live without any of these things. But there are two things we absolutely cannot do without. We cannot hope to survive without a glass of water and a piece of bread.

Kuttappan's Story

Not long ago, while driving in India with several of our brothers, I noticed something strange in the ditch on the side of the road. A closer look revealed a man lying there, completely motionless. I thought he was dead.

The driver of the car said, "Brother K.P., that man has been lying there for six days now."

"What?" I exclaimed. "Tell me what happened."

"Well," he said, "the man is an old beggar and has been living on the streets. Six nights ago he was hit by a car and broke his leg. No one wants to pick him up or even touch him. But an old lady comes every day and gives him some rice and a drink of water."

I was stunned. "If Jesus were to go by this place, what would He do?" I asked. The car grew silent.

When we arrived at our destination, I suggested we go to the police and ask for permission to pick up the old man and take him to the hospital. It was granted, and some of our brothers went to get him. They told me the rest of the story later.

The old man's hair looked as though it had never been cut, combed or washed. He had probably not washed his body in years. His clothing—more like rags—was so dirty it was black with grime. There is a type of ant that feeds on dead bodies, and thousands of these ants were eating away at his flesh. He had not been able to move since he was hit, and so he lay there in his own filth.

At the hospital the doctors and nurses tried to remove his clothes to give him a bath, but he kept fighting them. He clutched the rag he wore and wouldn't let go of it. Finally someone discovered that at one corner of his shirt there was a knot, and in the knot was a one-rupee coin (equivalent to about five

17

cents). He was holding onto this rag for dear life because he didn't want to lose his rupee! Once they handed him his coin, he relaxed and let go of his clothes.

As he got better, I went to the hospital several times to visit him and pray with him. I learned his story. His name was Kuttappan. He was seventy-five years old, and for as long as he could remember he had lived on the streets. They were his home. He had no knowledge of relatives, a wife, children or home.

Now let me ask you something. Did Kuttappan survive seventy-five years without our list of basic essentials? Yes, he did. A handful of rice and a glass of water from the old woman kept him alive.

We too could survive just as Kuttappan did. We would do just fine without any of our basic essentials. If you lived in a tropical climate, you could even survive without a stitch of clothing on your body— although perhaps not in public!

But there is no way you could live without bread and water.

Do you find anything in this life that is more important? Is there anything that carries even greater value than this most basic of essentials—something of higher priority than even a piece of bread and a glass of water?

Jesus thought so. Let's look at John 4 to see what was more important to Him than eating and drinking.

Lift Up Your Eyes

As we read through the Gospels and observe Jesus' life, we find that He constantly took every opportunity to teach His disciples about the kingdom of God. Whatever He taught, He lived it before them. Everything He said was clearly reflected in His life. He was a living, breathing example to His disciples. These twelve men had an opportunity to watch His life and learn from His every action.

One of these occasions that truly challenged and changed them is recorded in John 4. And it is as relevant for us today as it was for Jesus' disciples.

You are probably familiar with the story of the woman at the well and how Jesus spoke to her about living water. The disciples had gone into the city to buy food, and when they returned they offered it to Him.

"In the mean while his disciples prayed him, saying, Master, eat. But he said unto them, I have meat to eat that ye know not of. Therefore said the disciples one to another, Hath any man brought him ought to eat?

"Jesus saith unto them, My meat is to do the will of him that sent me, and to finish his work. Say not ye, There are yet four months, and then cometh harvest? behold, I say unto you, Lift up your eyes, and look on the fields; for they are white already to harvest" (John 4:31-35).

You can imagine how confused the disciples were! Jesus obviously had to be hungry from His journey, and so they walked to the nearby village to buy something for Him to eat. They hadn't eaten yet either and were probably just as hungry and thirsty as Jesus.

Then Jesus acted as if He'd already eaten. He told them, "I have food to eat that you aren't aware of."

This confused them even more.

"We went to all this trouble, and now He won't eat! Did anyone bring Him something to eat?" they asked each other. Maybe that was why He wasn't hungry.

What was Jesus really saying? He seized upon a normal, everyday event—eating—to illustrate to His disciples a principle of a completely different kingdom.

Then Jesus explained: "Listen, this is what I mean. You are horizontally oriented. You are thinking about the here and now—your tired and dusty feet, your growling stomach and your parched throat.

"But lift up your eyes! Pull your attention away for a minute. Look into eternity and see what I see. You say there are still four months before harvest arrives. But I tell you, look right now to the souls of men and women around you—the fields are already ripe and ready to be harvested! If you wait a little while longer, the crop will be gone—destroyed.

"Yes, I am hungry. I am thirsty. But the crisis out there is so real that it consumes all of My being. Compared to what is happening, I no longer have an appetite. I am desperate to finish what My Father has given Me to do."

Why did Jesus use food to explain kingdom principles? He could have used any number of things to make His point.

Perhaps it makes more sense to us this way. For us, the barest of necessities do not consist of anything but a glass of water and a piece of bread.

Jesus is saying this to us: "Even your most basic of essentials—bread and water—are not important to Me when I know of those who are dying right now without My Father's love."

Jesus speaks to us today just as strongly as He did to His disciples. He has given us the same command: "Follow Me." If we are to be called His followers, then we will do the same things He did.

As human beings, made of the same flesh and blood as the disciples, we are also horizontally oriented. We focus on the here and now—clothes, houses, education, bank accounts, styles, finances, cars.

But Jesus is calling us to lift up our eyes and look away from it all. He is calling us to see what He sees, to feel the urgency He feels, to share His heart for the harvest that will soon be gone—destroyed forever—if it is not reaped today.

Jesus lived with desperation. Throughout the Gospel accounts, urgency marked His life: "I must go," "He had to go through Samaria," "I must work ... night is coming," "You go and make disciples...." Phrases like these from Jesus' lips tell us how He felt and what He lived for. He was desperate—desperate enough that food and drink didn't matter anymore. How different this is from our casual, laid-back approach to life and our attitude toward the lost world!

How Can I Not Be Desperate?

Recently, newspapers in India carried the story of a Hindu man who, like many other devotees, embarked on a pilgrimage to a holy site to receive forgiveness for his sins. However, it was his desperate desire to be cleansed of sin that caught the eye of the media.

The man began his journey with his two sons, some two hundred kilometers from the holy mountain which was his destination. He took a small pebble in his hand and lay down on the dirt road, stretching himself out as far as he could reach and placing the pebble there. Then he raised himself up and walked to where the pebble lay. Picking it up, he went through the entire motion again ... and again ... and again. Body length by body length, he and his sons slowly made their way to the pilgrimage site.

At one point along a busy highway, a speeding truck hit one of the sons, killing him instantly. The man continued on his way, his passion for forgiveness greater than any grief he felt for his son.

"Nothing is too great a price to pay for my forgiveness," he told the news reporters who had gathered at the scene. "I am willing to do whatever it takes."

The man and his remaining son continued on the arduous journey until they finally reached the peak of the holy mountain. As they prepared to offer their sacrifice to the gods they worshiped, the man directed his son to turn away and begin to pray. The boy obediently complied. While he was looking the other way, his father took a knife and sacrificed this remaining son, in final hope for forgiveness of his sins.

A missionary leader later told me, "That man and his sons passed by on the road beside my house.... If I had seen them, I could've given them a tract and shared the gospel with them. Tell me, how can I *not* be desperate to reach my own people with the gospel?"

His question has echoed in my mind many times since.

Thinking in Terms of Eternity

Since the breakup of the Soviet Union, doors are opening for the gospel to reach into some of its remotest parts. Some of the new republics are nearly 100 percent Muslim. Who will win them to Jesus? They all need to be reached with the gospel—the Uzbeks, the Turkmens, the Azeris and millions of others.

The underground church is coming forward now, willing to send hundreds of their young people, well-schooled in suffering, to go and preach the gospel full-time. One of the leaders I have been in contact with has told me they urgently need our prayers and support to reap a harvest of souls that is ripe *today.*

However, the average Christian struggles to apply

these facts personally. It's much easier to spend our time and money on ourselves.

Perhaps a wife realizes her husband's birthday is coming up; she shops for something nice for him. She spots a silk tie and thinks, *Oh, that's a handsome one! He will really like it.* She picks it up and drops it in her shopping cart without even noticing the twenty-dollar price tag. One more tie to add to the dozens already in his closet!

Yet what will we do with information from the mission field about the needy men and women who are laying their lives down to reach the unreached with the gospel? When it comes to giving for missions, somehow we don't want to—or know how to—incorporate these facts into our everyday lives.

We must lift up our eyes. We need to retrain our minds to interpret everything we do, everything we see, everything we spend in the light of eternity—in the light of souls that are dying without Jesus.

I remember my first trip to China. One of the things I learned there that still boggles my mind is that there are multitudes of churches with hundreds, even a thousand members without one Bible in the entire congregation.

That twenty-dollar tie—did you know it could have purchased twenty Bibles, or twenty thousand gospel tracts? Add to this the fact that half of the world is still waiting to see the first page of a Bible, or any gospel literature for that matter.

Please Do Something

Recently, in one of our Gospel for Asia board meetings, the members of the board brought up the need for a safer car for my wife, Gisela. With the rise in car accidents and the vital part she plays in the ministry, both in North America and abroad, they felt strongly that we should invest in a well-built foreign model that had some wonderful safety features.

My wife was raised in Germany. She is not unfamiliar with many of the more expensive European cars—in fact, they were a common thing during her growing-up years. I thought perhaps she would see the wisdom of these suggestions and agree.

"Even if I were to ride in a tank," she replied, "that wouldn't stop an accident from happening. And when I think about our brothers on the mission field who don't even own a bicycle and have to walk ten, fifteen, twenty miles to preach the gospel, I don't feel comfortable buying an expensive car—even a used one. I don't want it. We will live with the car we have. That is good enough." Her reply didn't surprise me.

As I share my heart with you, I don't want you to come away with the thought that you have simply read another exposition on John 4.

Please do something about what you are reading! This is where lifting up your eyes—and living for Jesus—truly begins.

We are called to fulfill different tasks in the Lord's kingdom. Therefore, our response to His call will be as individual as we are. Some may hear the call to full-time missionary work. Others may sense the Lord directing them to pray for and send others. Some may make small changes in their external life-styles; for others, it may be a radical, revolutionary *coup d'état* of the heart.

Real for the First Time

Such was the case of one man who had just finished reading my first book, *Revolution in World Missions*. He was shaken out of his comfortable life-style by a major earthquake.

Early one morning I was awakened from a sound sleep by the telephone ringing. It was this brother calling me.

"I'm sorry to wake you, Brother K.P.," he said.

"It's no problem," I assured him sleepily. "Please tell me what's in your heart."

"Brother K.P., I didn't sleep at all last night," and his voice broke. I could hear him sobbing.

Finally he was able to talk again. "I want you to know a little about me. I live very well. I own my own business. I drive two Mercedes. My house is worth three quarters of a million dollars." He went on, listing the valuable things he owned. I listened.

"I am a born-again, Bible-believing Christian who goes to a fine church. But I just finished reading your book, and I am so broken, so torn up inside that I don't know what to do with myself.

"I want to be real for the first time in my life. I want to be able to live with myself. Just before I called you, I was on my knees before the Lord. I have decided that I am going to sell my house and purchase a smaller one. After all, it's only me, my wife and our child. I have decided to sell my two cars and buy something less expensive. And I am going to sell my fifteen-thousand-dollar watch and get a cheaper one." And he went on and on, listing the changes he wanted to make in his life-style.

"Brother," I told him, "I'm glad you called me. I pray that as the Lord has spoken to you about making all these changes, they will not be only a little anesthesia to keep you happy for a short while but that you will go the distance in obedience to Him." Then I prayed with him, and that was the end of our conversation.

A few months later I met a close friend of his. "How is he doing?" I asked.

The friend told me, "You wouldn't believe it if you saw it. He has sold everything! He is happily living a much simpler life and sharing with everyone why he has done it."

After reading this story, you may say to yourself, "Well, he was rich, and I am not. Besides, he had a lot of things to get rid of."

My friend, lifting your eyes from the things of this world is an activity that must begin *where you are.* Kuttappan, the old man who lay on the street for six days, was clutching onto his ragged piece of clothing for dear life. He wouldn't let the filthy thing go. Why? Because he didn't want to lose his coin.

What are you grabbing for? Whether it is a basic essential or a luxury, nothing is more important in God's heart than reaching the lost. Lift up your eyes, if just for a moment. Ask the Lord to lay His burden on your heart. Ask to share His perspective. See eternity stretching out before you.

Do you see any of the world's riches around the throne of God? No. But you do see multitudes—men and women and children that no man can number (Rev. 7:9).

Remember, millions of souls from every nation, tribe and kindred are still waiting to find out how they can come before the throne of God. We must see that vision of eternity and live our lives accordingly.

Jesus died for us that we may live. Let us lift up our eyes and see the harvest; and let us willingly live for others that they too may hear that He died for them.

In the next chapter, there are general guidelines to help you discover how to begin living in the light of eternity.

Chapter 2

Walking on the Road to Reality

As the plane began its final descent, flight attendants busied themselves picking up leftover meals, putting up tray tables and making sure we had our seatbelts fastened for landing. I found my thoughts wandering off, wondering what kind of people I would be meeting when I disembarked.

I wasn't sure what to expect. After all, Tim and Rachel (not their real names) were the ones who had called me a few months earlier and made a startling statement.

"Brother K.P., we want to give some money to your organization. But it's quite a large sum," said Tim.

"How much are you talking about?" I had asked him.

"One million dollars."

A million dollars! I had to ask again to make sure I heard him right.

During the course of our conversation, I learned that Tim worked as an electrician while Rachel stayed at home to care for their children. I couldn't help but wonder how they were able to give this kind of money away.

When I asked, Tim replied, "Brother K.P., as a family we live quite simply. The money we want to give is an inheritance."

"Is this all the money you have?" I asked.

"Yes, that's all of it," he answered.

"Tim, give me three days to pray about it," I said, "and I will call you back."

As I hung up, my heart was deeply troubled. This young couple planned to give away all they had—everything—to our ministry. Their trust in us was sobering. The weight of responsibility and good stewardship was heavy upon me. I could not handle the fact that we would be, in essence, taking everything from them.

I asked my staff to fast and pray with me about it. Three days later I called him back. I didn't feel a peace about taking the whole sum of money, I told him, but I felt the Lord giving us the freedom to accept an amount needed for one specific project about which we'd been praying—nearly $300,000. I also told him of other mission organizations he could contact and pray about helping, if God directed him to do so. A few days later their check arrived in the mail.

I was scheduled to be in their area to speak at a missions conference, and now I was also about to meet this couple for the first time. Tim and his wife came to pick me up at the airport for a time of fellowship.

Tim and Rachel were there, greeting me with

warm smiles. They weren't wearing anything that would reveal them as an obvious source of a million dollars. I didn't know what to think, but already my preconceptions were being blown away.

After a warm handshake, Tim led the way to their car. Now I was really in for a shock. We headed for an old, well-used station wagon, he loaded my luggage in the back and off we drove.

Tim's house was not grandiose by any stretch of the imagination and was quite simple in construction. Rachel was a gracious hostess, and their troop of small children played happily and noisily throughout the house.

As I spent more time with Tim and Rachel, I came to know their story. As a young, single man, Tim had spent much time with the Lord in prayer and in the Word. He became so moved with compassion for the lost world that it nearly broke his heart. Tim sold his house, his cars and most of the clothing he owned. He took the money from the sale of these items and quietly sent it off to many different countries, for the printing of gospel literature. He lived so radically for Jesus that some people actually thought he had gone crazy.

During this time he met Rachel. Before long they knew they were in love. However, Rachel came from a very wealthy family. Tim told her, "Even though I love you, I can't even think about marrying you."

"Why?" Rachel asked.

"You know I have given my entire life, my job, everything for one cause—to win the lost in my generation for the Lord. If I marry you, with the millions of dollars that come with your name, you may not want to live the life I have chosen. I can't marry you, Rachel."

"You don't understand, Tim," Rachel told him. "I

love you because of the way you are. This is the kind of life I want."

And so they made a pledge between themselves and the Lord: They would never touch one penny of the money that Rachel would bring to their marriage. Tim would continue his electrician's job to meet their basic needs. They would live as simply as possible, buying used clothing and driving used cars. And all of the money from Rachel's inheritance, as well as any extra money from his job, would go completely to the Lord's work.

I will never forget Tim and Rachel, their house, their car—the life-style they chose to live. I will never forget the look of complete contentment and joy I saw on their faces. What I saw in their lives was a deliberate choice to interpret everything in the light of eternity. I saw a conscious effort to evaluate their lives on a daily basis, continually asking themselves if their actions, their decisions, their purchases and their very lives were helping to reach the lost. I saw complete abandon and a willingness to walk down the road that leads to reality.

Discovering the Reality

So many believers today are searching for reality in their lives. They want some way to connect what they believe with what they live, but they don't quite know what steps to take.

How do we implement these principles into our lives? How do we become more eternally minded? How do we begin to live more simply and become more missions-conscious?

There are two dangers we must be careful to avoid. First, we can see the life Jesus asks us to live and become overwhelmed by what seem to be impossible demands. The result is *no action at all*—it's just too hard to do."

Second, a person can take the message of spiritual reality and translate it into *all action and no heart*. We can get whipped up into a frenzy of activity and supposed sacrifice that means nothing at all because it is not motivated by love.

I trust that the following guidelines will make your way clear as you seek the Lord for reality in your life.

1. *Go to the Word of God.* Anything that is in the realm of obedience to the Lord must be found in the Word. As you commit to open your heart to the Word of God on a daily basis, the Holy Spirit will take what you are reading and give you a personal application.

2. *Apply the truths from the Word of God to your own practical, personal realm.* Determine to take the Word of God personally. Ask yourself, How does this apply to me specifically, where I am now, and in regard to those with whom I am living and working?

In Matthew 16:24 Jesus says, "If any man will come after me, let him deny himself, and take up his cross, and follow me." Now ask yourself, What does it mean to deny myself and take up my cross today? How can I follow Jesus today? Wait before the Lord, and ask the Holy Spirit to reveal His truth to you.

I have found that obedience to the Lord is seldom a pleasant experience for my flesh. Most of the time I don't enjoy it!

A friend of mine once shared with me how he set his alarm clock a few minutes earlier in order to get up in the morning to pray. How he hated that alarm clock! A few times he really pounded it to shut the thing off. Sometimes he just buried his head in his pillow and went back to sleep again. If he did get up, he'd shuffle to the sink and splash some cold water on his face. And how he hated that cold water! And as he knelt by the bed to pray, he realized that this didn't feel good either.

Then, he told me with a chuckle, he began to realize that it really was working—he *was* waking up. His prayers *were* being answered, and he was drawing closer to the Lord.

We are not living in plastic shells like some ethereal, spirit-like vapor. We are made of flesh and bone. When we look at the cross where Jesus died, we see pain, agony, misunderstandings, loneliness, rejection, loss and even death. When the Lord asks us to take up the cross, to understand Christ and His fullness, we must personally accept inconveniences in our lives. It may mean fasting and praying, spending a long time in the Lord's presence, gathering the courage to tell someone about the Lord or rejecting the urge to buy an expensive shirt.

Your mind may argue with you and try to rationalize this all away. Your emotions may protest against the discomfort you have accepted. But deep within your heart you know that the Word of God is true, and that to obey, you must apply it to your life.

3. *Take the things you know to be right and implement those actions and decisions in your life right now.* Don't wait for some big revelation to appear to you in the night sky. Right now, begin to sacrifice, begin to pray, begin to fast, begin to witness, begin to repent, begin to ask for forgiveness from others when you wrong them. Start immediately to do the things *you already know* the Lord has told you to do.

As you continually walk with Him, the Lord will reveal more truths to you and shed more light on your life. Right now, begin to implement the meaning of the cross in your life.

We are all at different places in our walk with the

Lord. Something the Lord has called me to deny in my life may mean nothing to someone else. What you must do is take the knowledge the Lord has given you and do what you know to be the right thing. And, as I said before, the place to begin is in the Word of God.

4. *Whenever the culture or society around you becomes a hindrance to obeying the voice of God and the revelation He has given you in His Word, you must say no to it, no matter how impossible it seems.*

Daniel and his friends were taken captive into Babylon and were given the king's food as their daily provision. Now, it was considered a normal, wholesome, and acceptable custom to eat the food and drink the wine. Daniel had every reason to say to himself, *I'm in Babylon now, and my captivity has not happened without God's knowledge. I'm part of this society now—there is nothing wrong with eating and drinking what is set before me.*

But you see, Daniel had a greater revelation. It went beyond the culture of that day. And he chose to remain true to what God had revealed rather than to the culture. "But Daniel purposed in his heart that he would not defile himself ..." (Dan. 1:8).

We cannot conform to our culture if our obedience to the Lord is jeopardized in the process. We must realize that we will bear the responsibility for our walk with the Lord, not the culture in which we live.

Every culture perceives needs differently.

In India, for example, you will very rarely see pews or chairs of any kind in a local church. We sit on the floor to worship—it's just part of the culture. In the West we sit in pews or on chairs; it's part of the culture. Floors or pews—neither one is more spiritual; it is simply cultural.

Imagine for a moment that the leadership of a Western church decides that regular pews aren't good enough. They decide that pews must be replaced with individual, cushioned, reclining rockers—for more comfort! Now, that does seem a little outrageous. There is nothing wrong with worshiping God sitting in a pew, but there is no need to squander money on new seating when it could have been better used elsewhere to further the work of the Lord.

We must learn to distinguish between the dictates of culture and what the Lord is asking us to do.

5. *Each believer must be persuaded in his or her own heart.* Ultimately, we must each begin to move and act where we are. Nowhere in the Bible does it say that your all-out commitment to Christ means you have to take your family to some remote jungle area and die there. The call of the Lord is different for each individual. One day you will stand before the Lord and be called to give an account for the things He asked *you* to do.

The native missionaries who labor on the mission field are there because they heard God's voice telling them to go. They knew the troubles and trials before them. They saw the need, they heard the call and they obeyed. We must also be living in the same reality. When we hear God's voice, we must act accordingly and do whatever it is He is asking us to do.

Let me tell you this: A man can be a multimillionaire, own a huge business, and be more committed to Christ in His walk than someone who owns nothing and lives on the street. You must be persuaded in your own conscience that you are following the Lord's direction for your life.

As a matter of fact, it may be more difficult to stay behind the scenes as a sender than to go yourself. You are not on the front lines. You live simply, work a regular job, remain faithful to the Lord and preserve your testimony before all your coworkers. Then you take the money you have earned through your toil and sweat and give it to support a missionary in China or India or Bangladesh, someone you've never seen; you pray for him and support him faithfully. That is true sacrifice and living by faith.

You see, I cannot dictate to you a certain standard of living. There is no line that anyone can draw, culture or no culture. Each one must be persuaded to live before the Lord as he or she is led by the Lord.

6. *Don't be persuaded by guilt.* Never let anyone intimidate you or condemn your actions. Check yourself if you hear yourself thinking thoughts like this: *I'd be a better Christian if I did thus-and-so.... I feel bad about the house (or cars) I own.* I would advise that if you are motivated to do something out of guilt, don't do it.

God is not in the business of putting people on guilt trips to make them do something. He never condemns you!

He will call you on the carpet and ask you, with His great love, "Are you living by My standards?"

When Jesus spoke to Peter after His resurrection, He didn't say, "You creep, you rat. You denied Me, and now I'm going to get you." No! From just one glance Peter could tell that Jesus was saying to him, "Peter, I love you more than you could ever know. Forget the past—everything is forgiven. Now go and feed my sheep."

Whatever you hear, whatever you read, whatever challenges you—remember that your resulting actions should never be generated by guilt, flesh or carnality.

Purpose in your heart that you will never live by someone else's standard, but only by the things you know to be true from the Word of God and by the Holy Spirit teaching you daily as you are open to His leading in your life.

7. *Be on your guard for false humility (which is actually pride) and condemnation of others.* It is easy to read a book like this and think of "So-and-so, who really needs to hear this message!" It is always easier to see the speck in someone else's eye, even when there is a beam in your own.

Remember Jesus' sober warning in Matthew 7:1-2: "Judge not, that ye be not judged. For with what judgment ye judge, ye shall be judged: and with what measure ye mete, it shall be measured to you again."

No one can live a life that will satisfy everyone. We cannot be motivated to make changes in our lives simply because it will make us look good in our friends' eyes or because it will make our friends look bad. Pride can drive us to do illogical, unreasonable and downright stupid things.

I am so grateful for the staff God has given us here at our Gospel for Asia headquarters in Texas. If anyone asked me to describe the relationship we have, I'd describe us best as a family.

Our work and our lives are closely intertwined. We agonize for one another in prayer; we come to one another's aid in times of hardship or struggle; we rejoice together in victories in our own lives and on the field.

It would be so easy to look at one another's lives, comparing life-styles, salaries and convictions. To a certain extent, that is the temptation among any group of Christians. But we must remember that our commitment to one another goes beyond the eight to five workday. We must remember that we all serve the same Master. We all live with the same profound commitment to see the lost reached. And we all live with love for one another. Everything else becomes just incidental details.

We cannot expect each other to be perfect. But, at

the same time, our conscience and our walk with the Lord must be kept clear before both God and man. If we are following the truth from the Word, we will have no reason to fear condemnation from others, and neither will we desire to lord it over others as if we were more spiritual than they.

You Have to Sleep with Yourself

Sometimes, after I speak in a meeting, I feel somewhat troubled over what I said. Perhaps I was too strong, I think. Perhaps I made people feel guilty and drove them to legalistic bondage. But I know this is not my motivation at all.

My only desire is to stir up hearts to see the reality of what is going on beyond their own little horizons. There is a world out there that is dying and going to hell by the tens of thousands. All the Lord has asked me to do is to share His heart and give some practical solutions for becoming involved in His work.

Someday we will all stand before the Lord. Each one of us will be individually responsible for what we do with this information. Will we do our part to help reach our generation for Christ? Or will we pretend to ignore it, like a nagging alarm clock that woke us up too early in the morning?

You see, you are the one who has to live with yourself and the decisions you make. You have to sleep with yourself tonight.

Picking Up the Cross

The opportunities to do just what I've been talking about are plenty. Right now there are millions in unreached lands who are waiting to hear the gospel— and there are thousands of missionaries who are willing and ready to go. Perhaps the Lord has spoken to your heart to begin to support one of these needy brothers or sisters.

Perhaps the Lord is asking you to give up your job, your dreams of a comfortable life-style, that girlfriend or boyfriend—and go to the mission field yourself, investing a significant portion of your life for those who have never heard the gospel.

Sit back and consider what you have read. Begin to implement God's call on your life right now. Cut back on those unnecessary things in your life—the gum, the extra ice cream, those plans for buying another car. Yes, you're right—it doesn't feel good!

But you are beginning to pick up the cross. You are stepping out on the road to reality. And the consequences of a decision like this will last for all eternity. You won't regret it—I guarantee you.

Chapter 3

WHAT WILL YOU DO?

As I travel around North America, speaking in churches and home groups, I have learned that it is valuable to close my message with a time of questions and answers. Not only does my audience have a chance to ask or share what is on their hearts, but I am provided with a wealth of information on the state of the church at large.

On one such occasion in California, a young man stood up to ask a question. He was a university student, well-educated, and I could tell he was searching for answers.

"I just finished reading your book *Road to Reality*," he said. "You say some very hard things in this book. What I want to know is, how can I live out these principles that you talk about? I find it quite hard to walk away from this comfortable life I am so accustomed to living. Can you help me?"

As he spoke, I was already praying, "Lord, give me some way to answer this young man."

"Your questions tell me something about you," I told him. "You are troubled. You desperately want to do the right thing. You don't know what to do with this message, nor how to apply it. You know Jesus is asking you to sell out for Him, but you are looking for some emotional confirmation, some happiness to support your thinking. But you aren't finding any, are you?"

There was absolute silence in the auditorium. I realized that this young student was really the spokesperson for many others there that day who were facing the same struggles. They waited for me to go on.

Walking Away from It All

As I continued to share, the Lord reminded me about Abraham. I was browsing through a book on ancient culture recently and made some fascinating discoveries about ancient Ur in Mesopotamia, where Abraham came from. In the 1920s Sir Leonard Woolley, a British archaeologist, traveled to this area and studied the ancient city of Ur.

I told my audience that through many excavations, Woolley and his people learned that Ur was a very affluent society. Ur was a bustling port city through which many luxury goods traded hands, including precious stones, gold, timber and ivory.

Abraham lived in the midst of this affluence. Ur was his hometown. His family and relatives surrounded him. His life was secure and comfortable.

Yet he was different from those around him in one

significant way—he had a relationship with the living God. Everyone else was involved in heathen worship, but somehow Abraham knew God and worshiped Him.

Then God appeared to him and said, "Abraham! I want you to leave your father, your mother, your brothers, your sisters, your relatives, your land—everything."

"Imagine with me what it must have been like for Abraham to hear from God," I told the audience.

"'And then what, God? Where do You want me to go?'

"'I will show you.'

"'Leave *everything*? Even my parents?' Abraham's thoughts whirled in his mind. 'How can my family even begin to understand what I want to do? First of all, I worship a God who *talks* to me. They will think my mind is gone. Besides, family ties are so deeply ingrained in my culture; how can I even think of leaving my father and mother? They will think I have no respect for them whatsoever.'

"Abraham spent days wrestling with this call of God," I told my audience. "What the Almighty had asked him to do was not an easy thing. It went against everything he had been taught to value from childhood. It went against the very fiber of the community and culture. To obey this call would have some serious ramifications which he had to consider.

"We need to remember that we have the advantage of knowing the whole story. We can look back knowing all the facts. Abraham and those around him had no idea what was going to happen. There was no story in Genesis in which to discover the happy ending. There was *nothing*.

"One evening at dinner, Abraham was unusually quiet and subdued. His face, pale and drawn, showed the strains of his inner struggle.

41

"He was not unnoticed. 'What's wrong, Abe?' his father Terah asked. 'You haven't been yourself tonight, or lately for that matter. Something is on your mind.'

"Abraham swallowed hard. His mind was made up. It was time to tell them.

"'Father, I am leaving.' The words hung in the air and seemed to echo again and again in the heavy silence that followed.

"Finally, Terah spoke. 'You're—leaving? Where are you going?'

"All eyes were on Abraham as they waited for his reply.

"'I'm sorry, Father—I just can't tell you. You would not understand. All I know is that the God I worship has called me to leave everything here and follow Him. Please excuse me.' Abraham rose and walked out into the night air, glad for some relief from the intense atmosphere.

"His relatives and friends discussed Abraham's announcement late into the night.

"'The man has no respect for his parents, I'll tell you that much!' steamed one.

"'Abe is no dummy,' said another. 'I think he must've found a better place than Ur where he can strike it rich. That's why he won't tell us!'

"'No, something is troubling him—you can see that plainly,' a third responded. 'And he mentioned this God—which one does he mean? And have you heard that this God talks? Abraham says so. It makes me wonder if he isn't plagued with hallucinations.'

"'We will have more time with him tomorrow,' Terah broke in quickly. 'Let's all get some sleep tonight.'

"Tell me," I asked the group, "how could Abraham walk away from Ur, from wealth and security and comfort? For the rest of his life, we are told, he lived in tents. He lived in a strange country and was an alien and a pilgrim on the face of the earth. How could Abraham walk away from it all—his family, his friends, his home, his wealth?

"You will find your answer in Hebrews 11:10: 'For he looked for a city which hath foundations, whose builder and maker is God.'

"Later in Abraham's life, when he and Lot parted ways, he allowed Lot to choose the most fertile pasture land around. I'm sure Lot and his wife danced for joy at the sight of all they now owned.

"As Abraham walked away, I wonder what he was thinking. Later, the Lord came to him and said, 'Abraham, look up into the night sky. Do you see the stars there? I just said one word, and it all came into being. So shall your descendants be, Abraham.

"'Abraham, *I* am your reward.'

"Did Abraham know," I asked my audience, "that Ur, the city of wealth and prosperity that he willingly left behind, would someday crumble into dust and be buried under the shifting desert sands? Did he know that thousands of years later some British archaeologist would bring his shovel and rediscover Ur with all of its gold and silver?

"No, Abraham knew nothing of what was to come. But he did know one thing—there was a much better place on which he set his sights:

"'But now they desire a better country, that is, an heavenly: wherefore God is not ashamed to be called their God: for he hath prepared for them a city.... For here have we no continuing city, but we seek one to come'" (Heb. 11:16;13:14).

Leaving the Palace Behind

I thought, too, of Moses and the life of luxury he

willingly left behind in Egypt. Moses was raised in Pharaoh's courts as a prince. He had education, influence, power and wealth at his disposal. Yet he made a deliberate choice to walk away from it all.

When you think about his decision from a logical frame of reference, it makes no sense. I am sure those around him felt the same way.

Perhaps some of the Hebrews in slavery said to him, "Moses, what are you doing? Don't you realize you could be the key to our freedom? Just lay low, Moses. Don't rock the boat—stay in the palace, and someday soon we will overthrow all these Egyptians."

But Moses walked away from the luxury, the privileges, and the palace, and chose to become a shepherd. How could he give up all that he had? It looked totally illogical and unreasonable.

You will find the answer in Hebrews 11:27— *"seeing him who is invisible."* Years later, as he led the people of Israel through the desert and endured years of hardship along the journey, what kept him going? He could say, "I have seen Him who is invisible."

Moses would have been more justified than the rest of the Hebrews in desiring the good things of Egypt—the tasty food, the comforts and the securities—for he had experienced them all to the fullest. But he remained faithful, following the cloud by day and the fire by night. He lived a life that looked beyond the pleasures of his day and focused on the eternal I AM.

The reason these men could walk away from this world and all of its enticements was because they saw something that others could not. Eternity was stamped upon their eyes.

Life Is Too Short

World evangelism cannot be done by illusion.

Neither can it be done by manipulating others to perform spiritual-looking tricks.

World evangelism is accomplished by those who have abandoned their lives, obeying what Jesus said— "Forsake all and follow Me." It begins with an attitude of the heart.

Life is so short. There is no sense in investing our time, energies and finances into things that will soon burn up and be gone. Each morning as we awake, we must take a hard look at our lives in the light of eternity. We must ask ourselves, *What are the basics? What are the essentials I can live with*?

Yesterday Wasn't Good Enough

One evening not too long ago, I sat alone in a hotel room. The next day I would be speaking in a missions conference about living with the reality of a lost world. It was late, and I was tired. Instead of praying about the next day or going to bed like I should have, I switched on the television.

An episode of "Star Trek" was just beginning. Now, I must explain to you that I have always been fascinated by the futuristic gadgets this show portrays! So I sat back and watched it from beginning to end.

As I turned off the TV, I looked at my watch. It was already 11:30! I felt terrible for how I had wasted my time. *I can't believe I did this*! I said to myself. *I have to get up early and speak tomorrow*!

I was so disappointed in myself. Jesus stayed up all night too — but He *prayed!* My body is not made of steel, and I wear out if I try to go on just a few hours' sleep each night. I should have either been praying or sleeping, but instead I wasted a precious hour.

Then I realized that the devil was using my

45

mistake to waste even more of my time as I sat there and wallowed in my guilt and frustration.

I quickly knelt beside my bed, buried my head in the pillow and said, "Jesus, I know Your blood is sufficient to forgive me and cleanse me from my wrongdoing. Will You please do it?"

The accusing voice of the enemy whispered into my mind, "Are you stupid? How many times have you said that before?"

But I knew in my heart I had been forgiven. "One more time," I said. "Jesus said He would do it."

I went to bed with peace of mind and heart. I quickly fell asleep and woke the next morning feeling fresh and grateful for a brand-new day that Jesus and I would go through together.

My dear friend, every day we must make new decisions with the knowledge that yesterday wasn't good enough. We cannot stand on yesterday's triumphs, and neither can we mourn over its losses.

Jesus told us that if we want to follow Him, we must take up our cross *daily.* As we continue to focus on eternity, we must allow the cross to operate within us every day. As we do so, we will find our flesh brought into the light. We will see our human nature in its true state.

Time is running out. Hell is real. Heaven is real. Soon it will be too late—we *must* reach our generation with the gospel of Christ. World evangelism will be carried out by rational, sober-minded, unmovable soldiers of the cross. We are called to follow the example of Jesus, who fixed His eyes on the cross that was before Him and never turned to the right or to the left. For Jesus, reaping the harvest of souls was His reason for living.

The decision to live with the cross on a daily basis is a choice you must make. We read our newspapers, listen to the radio and watch TV, and every day before our eyes we see the poor, the unknown, the unheard dying millions. You will respond one of two ways: Either you will choose to ignore what you know or you will take up your cross and follow Jesus.

My question to you is, *How will you respond?* It is your decision—no one can make it for you. What will you do with what you know?

You Have Been a Long Time Coming

During the pre-Civil War days of the South, sanitary conditions were very poor. A plague came to a city and brought havoc with it. The city's death toll was climbing, and there was hardly a home that did not have sorrow or a vacant room.

In one very poor home, the disease came and did rapid work. Each family member was carried out, one after the other, shrouded in sheets, until only the mother and her five-year-old son remained.

He crept up on his mother's lap, his eyes wide and serious, and said, "Mother—Father is dead. My brothers and sisters are dead. What if you die? What will I do?"

What could she say? With that little face so close to hers, what could she say? She must be brave. She swallowed hard.

She was a Christian woman. She said as quietly and calmly as she could, "My boy, if I should die, the Lord Jesus will come and take care of you."

And that was quite satisfactory to him. He had been trained from the earliest to know and love the Savior. He knew how good He was. The boy went back to his playing on the floor, thinking, *It is all taken care of. If Mother should die, Jesus will come, and that will be all right.*

His question proved all too prophetic. The disease worked quickly in his mother, and soon she was carried away as well. He followed and saw where she was buried. He came back to the house, and in the midst of the hustle and bustle he was forgotten, left alone in the poor, humble home.

He tried to sleep that night but couldn't, so he got up and dressed himself as best he could. He found his way to the cemetery where they had laid his mother. Finding the spot, he threw himself upon the fresh earth. Sleep came quickly.

Early the next morning a Christian gentleman was coming down the road from some errand of mercy that had kept him out all night. He came along the road past the graveyard and saw the boy, quickly imagining some kind of heartbreaking story. He called out, "My boy, what are you doing here?"

The boy raised himself, rubbed his eyes and said, "Well, my father is dead. My brothers and sisters are dead. And now my mother is dead. And she said that if she died, Jesus would come for me. And He hasn't come. I'm tired of waiting."

The man swallowed hard and then said very quickly, as he tried to control his voice, "Well, my boy, I have come for you."

The boy looked up at the gentleman with wide eyes and said, "You have been a long time coming."

As I write these words, there comes before my eyes a vision. This vision is with me day and night. It never goes away—and I don't want it to. The vision is of a great sea of faces from Africa, Turkey, Iran, the Middle East, Bhutan, Myanmar, Japan, China, India. I see a great cloud of faces with eyes that are searching and sad. They are hungry, empty and crying out, "You have been a long time in coming."

No Easy Road

What will you do? The choices and decisions you make will affect the course of your life forever.

Some of you will sell your large house in order to purchase a smaller one and begin to live more simply. Some of you will sell your diamond rings and jewelry and give that money for missions.

Some of you will take the money you are saving for the future and say, "I will live by faith. There is nothing worse than death, and life is not mine anyway—it is His."

Some of you will look at your job in a new light. It will no longer be the most important thing in your life but simply a means to do whatever you can to extend God's kingdom as you walk through this life. One doctor tells me often, "The reason I am a surgeon is simply because I know I can help to support missionaries who are winning thousands to Jesus." A carpenter says, "Brother K.P., the only reason I work so hard at my job is so I will be able to support the work of the Lord."

Some of you will go to the mission field yourselves, in obedience to the call of the Lord. You will choose to give up the comforts and conveniences that others enjoy. You will make a deliberate decision to live inside another culture and society so that others can hear the gospel.

I don't know which decisions and choices you will make. There are many to be made. You must begin where you are, with your eyes upon Jesus.

I offer you no easy road. I cannot challenge you to do anything that I have not done myself. When I began to make choices to live in the light of eternity, the Lord came to me with a sharp knife and said, "Son, here is the knife. You have to do the surgery on yourself. I can't do it for you."

We will struggle with uncertainty, self-pity, sorrow and agony. We will have to face criticism and misunderstanding from others. We will be strangers and pilgrims on this earth, just as Abraham and Moses were.

But I know one thing: My eyes are fixed on eternity—and the millions of souls that I want to bring with me. I don't compare my life with someone else's. I compare my life with what Jesus said: "Forsake all and follow Me." Jesus has never asked me to do something that He didn't do. I will follow Him.

A Rational and Sober-minded Choice

It is my sincere prayer that as you come away from reading this chapter, the devil will not take these thoughts and "immunize" you so that your heart is hardened to change.

May the Holy Spirit give you the ability to see that vision of faces who are crying out for life. May He give you that eternal perspective, and may He give you the burden for souls who are perishing.

The decision you make must be a rational, sober-minded one. Romans 12:1 says that presenting ourselves as a living sacrifice is our "*reasonable* service."

It is the Lord who must tell you what you must do with your life, your time and your resources. All I can give you are examples and illustrations.

Take time to be quiet before the Lord and listen to His voice. I pray that you make time each day to get to know Him and share His heart.

Chapter 4

GIVING OUR CHILDREN THE BEST WE KNOW

Nearly forty years ago an elderly Christian woman in Wyckoff, New Jersey, began a lonely, eighteen-year prayer vigil.

She lived near a busy high school, and she often watched the teenagers come and go.

She knew from her observations that one of the most difficult boys was a kid named George. Dorothea Clapp began to pray faithfully and daily for his conversion.

She prayed for George and sent him a copy of the Gospel of John. Two years later he did come to Christ. As he continued to grow, Mrs. Clapp prayed for his spiritual development.

George began to witness to his classmates. Over 125 came to Christ as a result. Later, as a college student, George made trips into Mexico with a group of friends who shared his heart for the lost.

Gradually the Lord expanded their vision to include nearly sixty other countries: England, Italy, Turkey, India.... Eventually his zeal led others to fan out across the world and start youth mission movements in many nations.

One of these witnessing teams came to India and visited my village when I was only sixteen, still barefoot and unable to read or write English.

The team challenged me to take the gospel north to the lost millions of Rajasthan, the Punjab and the Himalayas. You know the rest of the story, don't you? Today, as a result of the vision the Lord placed in my heart during that time, Gospel for Asia is able to sponsor thousands of full-time missionaries in eleven Asian nations. And mine is only one of the many lives that have been touched.

That young man's name was George Verwer, and as a result of Mrs. Clapp's prayer and interest in his salvation, millions have heard the gospel through Operation Mobilization. And out of OM, hundreds of alumni have started other churches and missions in many parts of the world.

The Example We Present

What if Mrs. Clapp hadn't taken the time to pray daily for George? What if she hadn't witnessed to him and encouraged him?

There is a whole generation of young people today who are looking for influences and examples to follow. Believe me, they will find someone to imitate. If we as parents and concerned believers do not accept the challenge, our children will find someone else.

The younger generation is faced with a choice

today: to follow the Lord with all their hearts, or to live for themselves just like the rest of the world. One of the greatest tragedies parents can experience in life is watching their children make wrong choices. It grieves me that multitudes of kids today are headed down the wrong road.

Why are so many of our children growing up in this way? Why are they so attracted to the values of this world and show little or no interest in spiritual matters?

Perhaps we need to look at ourselves for some answers. As parents, youth leaders or simply friends, we in the body of Christ need to present an example before our children that they will want to follow.

I will never forget my experience at a youth group meeting where I shared my heart and presented the challenge of world evangelism to a rather sizable group of high-schoolers.

As I closed the meeting, I appealed to them to carefully consider the claims of Jesus. I challenged them to make a decision about the lordship of Christ in their own lives. During a time of prayer, I asked those who were ready to follow the Lord to raise their hands. "If you want to share the Lord's heart and burden for the world by giving your life to reach the lost, let me see your hand," I said.

I was astounded to discover that not one single young man or woman was willing to make the commitment. No one even spoke to me afterward. I was soon to learn why these young people were so callous and indifferent to the claims of Christ on their lives.

Following the meeting, the youth director offered to drive me back to my room. He led me out in the parking lot to his luxurious sports car. As I sank into the rich leather seat, I was enveloped with loud music coming from the high-tech tape deck. The dashboard and controls reminded me of an airplane cockpit.

We took off like a rocket, and I was startled by his high speed and recklessness. "Don't worry," he smiled, "I have everything under control."

But as we proceeded to break every speed limit, I wasn't so sure. I felt spiritually ill at ease.

A single young man in his late twenties, the youth director chatted amiably with me about his career goals and plans. His remarks were sometimes serious, sometimes filled with ridicule—a mixture of flesh and spirit that contradicted each other from one moment to the next. During our conversation I learned how little he understood about surrender to Christ and the importance of a personal devotional and prayer life.

Then I understood why the youth of this church were so indifferent to the things of God. Here was a youth director who was barely more mature in the Lord than the young people he was hired to lead.

The Law of Spiritual Reproduction

Like always begets like. This is the most basic rule in propagation of any species—and in discipleship as well.

Here was a young man, undoubtedly chosen by the church leadership because he was popular with the youth. He planned a full round of social activities for them and kept them busy all the time. I am sure the parents and leadership in the church reasoned to themselves that this young man was earning the respect of the youth. They probably believed he had many chances to witness to them about the things of the Lord.

But what kind of witness and example did he offer? His irresponsible pattern of life was not committed to the things of God but to the ways of the world.

Surely all youth directors are not like this young man. I thank God for those who have taken their call seriously and are serving as unto the Lord.

Nowhere for the Kingdom

Unfortunately, it doesn't take many hours of traveling to come across parents, pastors, youth directors and others in leadership who practice this same life-style before multitudes of children and young people, who soak up their example like sponges.

One young man in particular comes to mind. I'll call him John. What happened to him occurs too often in our churches today.

As a high school student, he heard the call for world evangelism at a summer youth camp. He came home to his church-going parents and announced that he was giving his life for missions.

For a while they didn't treat his new vision for the world too seriously. They were impressed by his newfound zeal for the Lord but were also certain he would give up the idea in time. But John didn't grow out of it—at least, not at first.

As he entered his final years in high school, John began ordering information from Bible schools rather than respectable colleges. His parents started to panic. Was he really thinking of going to one of those unaccredited institutes? And what good would it do him in the real world?

They met with their pastor and asked him to help their son see how he was throwing his life away by becoming involved in full-time missions.

The pastor agreed to meet with John and invited him to come over to his office for career counseling.

"You know, John," said the pastor gently, "I was just like you when I first heard the call to the ministry. In fact, at first I wanted to go into missions too.

"But I learned—and you will too—that if God is really calling you to do something like that, then there's plenty of time. And your mom and dad are right to be concerned that you get a good education first. If your missionary service doesn't work out for one reason or another, then you'll always have something secure to fall back on."

He went on to stress family concerns. "Have you thought about your future wife and the children you may someday have? Have you given any consideration to the emotional and physical adjustments they must make to a harsher way of life?"

After the pastor explained some of the other risks and dangers involved in a missions career, he pointed to the diplomas hanging on his walls. "Get a good education first, John. I suggest you enroll in the best liberal arts college you can. Then, if you are really serious, you can go on to a good seminary and get your Masters of Divinity, or even a doctorate.

"You also need to get some experience working in our churches here at home. I have connections in other churches, and you can count on me to help you.

"Then, if you still want to go into missions, you'll know it's the real thing."

It all seemed to make sense to John, and everyone in his town was giving him the same sort of "slow down" advice. Besides, his girlfriend's parents were just as strongly opposed to the idea. They were respectable people, and they didn't want their daughter to have just a Bible school education—or perhaps marry someone who didn't have "a regular job."

If John went to college first, then she could enroll too, with the help of her family, and the two wouldn't have to be separated. John figured this would give her some time to see how important the missions call was in his life.

He wrote to several mission organizations that year, since he was still planning to go overseas for short-term missions work as a summer volunteer.

But after a year on campus, John decided to switch to a business major—everyone said that was where the future would be in society. After that, he never found the time to go overseas—not even short-term.

His girlfriend soon enrolled at the same college, and when she was in her third year, they married. However, two years later the marriage ended in a bitter divorce.

John's parents were heartbroken and realized that their interference had taken their son away from God's plan for his life and put him on a fast track to nowhere—at least nowhere for the kingdom of God.

But by then it was too late. John was already pursuing a graduate degree. There was no more talk of the Lord and the mission field now—he was too busy sending his résumé to top business firms.

John, of course, never went on to seminary or Bible school. Today he is in a successful business. He is now remarried and building a comfortable life for his family—complete with debt, a lavishly furnished house, two cars and a boat. To pay the bills, both he and his wife work. He still claims to be born again and attends church when it doesn't interfere with his career.

Where Does the Change Begin?

Sadly, in our churches today we find millions of men and women just like John. In their young, formative years they heard the call of God on their lives—but somehow were not given the direction they needed to respond properly.

There is no guarantee that without his parent's intervention John would still have gone on in missions. It is futile to ask What if?—yet, still, I wonder. Perhaps his burden for the lost would have resulted in his staying home after all and becoming a sender rather than a goer. However, today John is neither.

The world is ready to offer a substitute to our children: security, prestige, wealth and power—and total ineffectiveness for the kingdom of God. But it doesn't have to be that way.

Where does the change begin? It begins in our churches, in our youth group meetings, but most of all in our homes. If we can model for our children a life-style that is consistent with what we believe, I assure you we can reach our generation for Christ.

As we walked across the grounds of a Hindu temple, our son Daniel, only three at the time, was immediately attracted to a little baby girl crawling around on the stones. He tried to take a picture of her with his toy camera.

Instead, we placed them side by side and took a picture of them together with our real camera. As I look at that picture today, I notice not only the little girl's torn and dirty dress but also an amulet, tied around her neck with a string. Her parents were Hindus, and the amulet was to protect her from evil spirits.

Today I look at my children and am amazed at how much they've grown, and how fast time has flown since the days when they toddled around the house. Gisela and I love them dearly, and there is no doubt that we want the very best for them.

These Hindu parents loved their little girl as well, and they wanted the best for her. Unfortunately, the best they knew was an amulet to ward off evil spirits. They did not know that all the evil in the world has already been defeated. They did not know that Christ died and rose again so that all might be saved.

More than half the population of India is made up of children under the age of sixteen. The little girl we saw that day is one of millions of children who may never hear about Jesus before they die.

I tell you this in all seriousness: What you and I give to our children today will determine what these children and future generations will receive.

Imparting a Burden to Our Children

In light of this reality, I want to offer a few suggestions that will help you impart a burden for the lost world to the children and young people in your life. Your life, rather than your words, will be the greatest teacher.

Teach them from early on to love Jesus above all others. Jesus said in Luke 14:26, "If any man come to me, and hate not his father, and mother, and wife, and children, and brethren, and sisters, yea, and his own life also, he cannot be my disciple."

Nothing is to come between us and our relationship with Jesus. If children learn from the start to put Him first, before everything and everyone, they will be freed in advance from impure relationships and ungodly marriages.

If Jesus is first in a young person's life, it will automatically follow that every decision he or she makes will be bathed in prayer. If Jesus is first, we can come to Him with any request or concern.

When your children ask you for new clothes or the newest style of shoes, take the opportunity to ask, "Why don't we ask Jesus about it?" Teach them to take their requests and desires to Jesus.

My daughter Sarah had an opportunity to

experience this recently. To her dismay, she found a wart growing on her arm. It showed no signs of stopping, and it embarrassed her terribly. She began to wear a bandage over the wart to cover it up.

Gisela sat down with her one day. "Sarah," she said, "I want to tell you something. Jesus is the same yesterday, today and forever. Jesus healed people before, and He can heal us now. He answers prayer—you know that, Sarah. He has answered so many of the prayers you have prayed."

"Yes, Mommy, I know," Sarah replied. "But this?"

"Sarah, Jesus can answer your prayer and take your wart away too."

"You really mean that, Mommy?"

"Yes, Sarah, I really mean that."

So Gisela and Sarah prayed together and asked Jesus to remove the wart from Sarah's arm.

"Sarah," Gisela told her, "from today on, you will begin to see that wart getting smaller and smaller. Soon it will dry up and fall off."

And so they began to watch Sarah's arm day after day; and they saw the wart slowly shrivel up in answer to their prayer.

A few weeks later I was in my study, working on something, when Gisela came in. Sarah followed, with a shy grin on her face. "Sarah," her mother said, "why don't you tell Daddy what happened."

Sarah rolled up her sleeve, smiling even bigger. The wart had disappeared.

When you think about it, we expect certain routine things from our children: We expect them to bathe, brush their teeth, go to school and do their homework. These are not unreasonable demands—we see them as a basic part of living.

But when it comes to prayer and spiritual things, we slack up a bit. After all, we don't want to force them into legalism or bondage, we reason. What we fail to realize is that making Jesus part of a child's everyday life is even more basic and vital to living than learning to brush your teeth!

Teach your children to die to themselves. "If any man will come after me," Jesus said, "let him deny himself, and take up his cross, and follow me" (Matt. 16:24). Jesus made it clear that death to our dreams, hopes, expectations and fears is the qualification for any Christian.

There is an unwritten rule in today's society that if we let our children face the disappointments and dashed hopes that naturally come in this world, then we are somehow poor parents. Even in the Christian subculture we are taught to push our children to make goals and meet them, to pursue dreams and to satisfy the desires of a fleshly heart.

But what does *Jesus* ask of us? To die to it all. He doesn't want us to somehow fit Him into our busy schedule. He wants us to come to Him with no plans, no goals and no agendas. He wants us to come to Him with an open calendar, an open life, ready for Him to arrange our schedule as He sees fit in the work of the kingdom.

Did you know that pursuing the values set by our culture is a learned attitude? We can teach our children to "unlearn" them as well. We can also provide an atmosphere at home where they are never learned in the first place. When children see their parents approaching each day with a fresh dependence on the Lord for their plans and hopes, they too will learn to take up their cross daily.

Teach your children to forsake all. "Whosoever he be of you that forsaketh not all that he hath, he cannot be my disciple" (Luke 14:33).

In a world dominated by ever-increasing

materialism, no command seems harder to accept today than this one. Citizens of some of the most affluent nations in the history of the human race still cannot be satisfied with what they have. We live in an age where acquisition of wealth and financial security has become a favorite pastime.

The love of material goods—clothing, homes, insurance, properties, recreational toys, automobiles—is one of the greatest hindrances to world evangelism today.

It will be our attitudes and perspectives as parents and leaders that will influence how our children see these "things" that everyone else runs after. Jesus has asked us to forsake all if we want to follow Him. Before our children are able to do so, we must set the example.

Teach them to live a life of discipleship. For so many, being born again is the end of their spiritual life, not the beginning. They have failed to understand—and thus teach their children—that the Christian walk is an ongoing experience of daily submission to the Lord.

Walking with Jesus is not an easy road. Jesus called us to follow in His footsteps—and He was mocked, beaten and ultimately killed to save the world. Unless children and young people learn early on what this means, they will be blown away when the first fiery trial of their faith comes.

These truths are taught on every page of the New Testament, but somehow we have managed to lock away these realities of the Christian life. Young people who are serious about following Jesus need to understand that persecution and misunderstanding come to those who put Christ first. Suffering comes with the job. Sacrifice will always be needed if we are to reach the unreached with the gospel.

I do an enormous amount of traveling. This, of course, means I am gone from home quite often, and Gisela bears much of the responsibility for parenting Daniel and Sarah.

To this day my children have never heard their mother complaining or grumbling about my being gone. When they are sad or when they complain themselves, she draws them close and says, "It is our privilege to send Daddy out, so that Jesus can use him to help reach the lost." While we all feel the pain of this sacrifice we have chosen to make, my children are not bitter in the least.

Train your children to witness and share with others about Jesus. Young people can develop a burden for the lost at an early age simply by reaching out to those around them who don't know the Lord.

They can learn to reach out to friends at school and in the neighborhood. They can work with the deacons in your church to call on the sick, become involved in prison ministries and visit those who are in need.

As a parent or youth leader, you can take your children and young people on short-term mission trips to nearby needy areas.

But, remember, the best training for witnessing will come from you. As they observe you in your daily life, interacting with unsaved neighbors and friends, your children will learn to share the love of Jesus as well.

Make good use of available resources and materials. Obtain a world map and put it up in a prominent location in your home. Begin to pray as a family for missionaries you know of, and ask the Lord to direct your giving.

Read together from missionary biographies. There are numerous wonderful volumes available on the lives of men and women like Amy Carmichael, Jim Elliot,

Sadhu Sundar Singh, Hudson Taylor, William Carey and many others. Books like *Operation World* list prayer needs for each country in the world. Encourage your children to pray personally for a specific country or ethnic group.

Obtain the names and addresses of the missionaries your church supports. Make it a family project to learn about the countries they live and work in. Learn as much about their lives and needs as possible; and pray for them. Take the opportunity to invite visiting missionaries to your home. Gather your children around you and encourage them to ask as many questions as possible.

Don't Let Them Miss Out

The other day Daniel was getting ready to go with some of his friends to a free Christian music concert. He was not planning to take any money at all, but when I heard it was free I told him, "Son, you should at least take five dollars for the offering. It may be free to you, but someone has to pay for it."

Then I added, "Daniel, maybe you should take a little more money too, in case you find a T-shirt, or in case of an emergency."

My son's response stopped me in my tracks and taught me a lesson I will never forget. "Daddy," he said, "I don't want to take any more money. I'm not going to buy anything. My friends buy all these things, but it's just a waste of my money—I don't want it."

His statement was not a casual one. He knew what he was talking about. I remembered another incident earlier in his life when he had saved up a considerable amount of money, and he had been eyeing a special toy for quite some time. He finally had enough money, and it was only a matter of going to the store and making the purchase.

The next day my son came to me and said, "Daddy, I decided not to buy it."

"Why, Daniel?" I asked, puzzled.

"Daddy, last night after you prayed with me, I thought about this toy, and I thought about the thousands of people in India who don't have a Bible. I want my money to go to buy Bibles to give to those people."

Now why did my son make a choice like that? Neither Gisela nor I forced him into that decision. It was simply because, by the grace of God, he saw in our lives what we believed and lived for.

There is no instant solution that I can offer you. All you can do is live your life before your children, daily coming to the Lord and depending on His strength and grace to be the example that they will follow and imitate.

Don't underestimate your children's ability to understand the reality of the lost world. Give them the opportunity to experience what you are living for.

Commit yourself to praying daily for your children, that the Lord would save them and call them to serve Him.

There is an abundance of material things that we could easily give our children. But they are as useless as the amulet tied around that little girl's neck.

The best thing we can give them is Jesus. Teach your children about His love and His heart. Teach them to follow Him, to lay down their lives to reach the lost. Don't let your children miss out on the best you can offer them.

Living in the Light of Eternity

PART II

IN THE BATTLE ZONE

Living in the Light of Eternity

Chapter 5

KNOWING THE ENEMY

Now that you know what it means to break free from watered-down, plastic Christianity, you also need to know that your life now makes a powerful impact on the spiritual world.

Imagine, if you will, that you and I are allowed to observe a meeting held for all the powers of darkness. The setting is in a huge conference hall, and in the audience are millions of demons, gathered from all corners of the earth by Satan himself.

As they enter the hall, there is complete silence. They whisper to one another, "What is going on? What is this meeting all about? What is our Master's agenda?"

They look around, and there on the wall in huge letters are written these words: **"AND THIS GOSPEL**

OF THE KINGDOM SHALL BE PREACHED IN ALL THE WORLD FOR A WITNESS UNTO ALL NATIONS; AND THEN SHALL THE END COME" (Matt. 24:14).

Then the prince of darkness approaches the podium. His message to his army is based on these words from Jesus Christ. "Do you understand that when this gospel of our Enemy is preached to the whole world, it means *our* end as well?" he thunders.

You see, Satan is keenly aware of what will happen to him and his legions of demons when the end of time comes. He already knows what is written in the final chapter. He will be forever chained in the lake of fire. It is only a matter of *time* before the appointed, fixed moment when their doom will be sealed by God.

When Jesus was about to cast the demons out of the men in the country of the Gergesenes, the demons cried out, "What have we to do with thee, Jesus, thou Son of God? art thou come hither to torment us *before the time*?" (Matt. 8:29).

All the enemy has is a little time, which will be cut even shorter by the preaching of the gospel to all nations. As we reach our generation for the Lord, we will hasten His coming as well as the demise of the devil. If we are able to mobilize the entire body of Christ all over the world to move out and witness, it will only be a matter of a few years before Jesus returns.

Do you think the devil is happy over this fact? No. In fact, we are told he is full of "great wrath, because he knoweth that he hath but a short time" (Rev. 12:12). I can assure you that he does his utmost to extend that *time* in any way possible.

In the Heat of the Battle

For those of us who have committed ourselves to

70

pray, give and go to reach the lost world, this means that whether we realize it or not, we have set ourselves up for direct, face-to-face confrontation with the powers of darkness.

For years now at Gospel for Asia, whenever someone has been called to join our staff, we have made it a normal procedure to tell them right up front, "Now that you have made a decision to join this ministry, we want to put you on the alert that there will be many battles to face. You will experience attacks and opposition to your decision. You need to be prepared and pray that the Lord will protect you."

We have seen time and time again how those who are preparing to join our home team staff have faced serious attacks once they make their decision to come. Some have experienced health problems. Others have had to deal with emotional turbulence. And most face opposition, sometimes severe, from relatives and friends.

The battle we face with the powers of darkness is an ongoing one. If there is anything good to be said about the devil, it is that he is a hard worker. He never rests, he never sleeps, he never goes on vacation. He works all the time.

As long as our hearts are committed to serving the Lord and helping to advance His kingdom on earth, we will always face opposition from the enemy.

Not too long ago I received an early-morning call from George Verwer, international director of Operation Mobilization. He was in the middle of a trip, waiting for his flight in the airport, so he called me to share a few things on his heart.

We talked for some time about the things the Lord was doing all over the world, and then he said something that has remained fresh in my mind ever since: "You know, K.P., when I think of all that is happening on the mission field right now, Satan must have put you and Gospel for Asia as a number one target on his hit list right now."

"Well, George," I responded, "all I can ask you to do is please pray for us. We know the battle is real."

When we are involved in serving the Lord, especially when it comes to reaching people who live in lands ruled by demon powers and principalities for centuries, you can be sure that we will be in the very heat of the battle. We are a major threat to the enemy.

Supernatural Networking

Recently I heard of five hundred Hindu converts in North India who gave their lives to Christ and were baptized after watching a film on the life of Jesus.

Imagine what a stir this caused among the ranks of demons who suddenly lost their power over these people. Here's a possible scenario:

"What is wrong with you?" a demon leader demands of his gang. "Why did you let this happen?"

"Well, what can we do?" they whine. "We were doing our best to keep them in darkness, but these missionaries brought this projector and film in, and they keep going from village to village with it. And they do so much praying! They don't give us any rest!"

So the head demon checks out this Gospel for Asia outfit and finds out that somewhere in America—in Carrollton, Texas—funds are being raised to support these missionaries.

Suddenly the commander of the Carrollton region is alerted: "There is a group of people in your territory who are causing us big trouble in India! Do what you can to stop them!"

Soon the commander of these demons has a file on each of our staff. He knows each name, each address.

He knows every car that is driven and every book that is read. He knows each weakness, each fear, each struggle and how each staff member can be attacked the most effectively.

Does this sound a little outlandish to you? I discovered recently that anyone in India—even in the remotest village— can get CNN. All they have to do is pay to get it hooked up. I also found out that soon cellular telephones may be used anywhere in India or any Asian country.

Believe me, if man with his finite, low-level mind has the genius to get this type of network going, there is no doubt that Satan can make a connection between the things that happen on the mission field and your commitment to give and pray for missions.

Satan's ultimate goal is to do everything in his power to lead men and women away from Christ and take them to hell. Jesus calls Satan "the prince of this world" (John 12:31). The apostle John tells us that the whole world is lying in the lap of the wicked one (1 John 5:19). Political systems, religious hierarchies, financial institutions, educational and banking systems—everything in this world is easily manipulated by the enemy to lead men and women away from the living God and keep them in bondage.

Just as you will sometimes experience tensions and conflicts with those who are closest to you—your children, your spouse, your close relatives—you will also find a natural tendency toward friction in your church, in the Christian organization you work with or in your prayer group or home fellowship. Because we are living and working together as human beings, these things naturally occur.

The soldiers who go to war are the ones who get wounded. The families who have children are the ones who have struggles in raising them. Those who drive cars are the ones who have accidents. Those who are alive are the ones who get headaches and illnesses. Only if you are dead, lying there in your coffin under the earth, will you face no problems!

Jesus had plenty of problems with His disciples. They squabbled among themselves as to who was the greatest, and they fought for their future positions around His throne. Peter ran off at the mouth without thinking. Judas was ready to do anything for money— even betray his Master.

Somehow, in the process of doing our very best to build the Lord's kingdom, we will still face problems. We can expect it.

I want to point out four areas where the enemy can easily attack those whose hearts are committed to reaching the lost world. I want to share these because I believe that as you take these to heart and are forewarned, you will be strengthened and encouraged to stand firm in the days to come.

Burning the Barn Down

One attack of the enemy we face is *the temptation to major on minor issues*. For those who are in any way involved in winning the lost world, the attack of the enemy is much more severe and direct. He will take advantage of these problems we face and, like a balloon, blow them up bigger and bigger so that our vision of everything else is blocked. Suddenly, all we see are the problems.

I heard about a Christian organization that was attacked severely in the press. The problems stemmed from disagreements and misunderstandings between a couple of board members and the leader of this organization. The people who put fuel on the fire were so-called Christian brothers who went to the secular media with their complaints and undermined the work of God. The one negative thing was publicized; but no mention was made of the other ninety-nine good things this organization does.

The enemy used these men to blow the problem out of proportion. Not only did the annual income of this organization drop nearly one million dollars, but great damage was done to millions of suffering people around the world as a result.

This is what Satan does—he takes small things and makes them big. In a church, for instance, the pastor may have done something or said something that caused a misunderstanding. All of a sudden a clique is formed, people talk and blow the whole thing out of proportion and the church is divided instead of dealing with it.

Some time ago a woman called Gospel for Asia and told me that she and her husband could no longer support our organization. When I asked why, she said it was because someone had told her that GFA had become liberal. I asked how she had come to such a conclusion.

"Well," she responded, "I found out that GFA workers do not use the King James Version of the Bible."

"I'm sorry, they don't," I replied.

"You have deceived me!" she exclaimed. "I can't support your work any longer."

Then I asked her, "Are you aware that your missionary who is working in Thailand doesn't speak English? You realize, of course, that the King James Bible is in English?"

My point here is not to argue about the King James Version. I use it myself and always have. But you see what happened? This woman took a small problem and blew it out of proportion. In the process she had decided to give up her commitment to support native missionaries. (After we talked further, she decided to continue supporting them.)

The enemy will point out and highlight specific failures— even the smallest things, of those with whom you work and fellowship —pastors and elders in the church and leaders of Christian organizations. When this happens, be on your guard against focusing in on just that problem alone. You cannot see the total picture if you are doing this. You will become blind. And this can be very dangerous.

If you were to take a large balloon and blow it up enough, your sight would gradually become blocked. The balloon looms larger and larger in your vision as you continue blowing. Eventually all you would see is the balloon.

Even Jesus encountered this. The Pharisees caught His disciples eating their food without washing their hands according to the Jewish law. They blocked out everything else Jesus taught and focused in on this one apparent failure. When Jesus healed the sick on the Sabbath, the Pharisees jumped on Him and said He couldn't be from God since He worked on the Sabbath. These Pharisees were extremely conscientious when it came to religion. They gave tithes, prayed and fasted, but they left out mercy, kindness and love.

There seems to be an increasing tendency today for believers to search out the smallest hint of anything negative in Christian organizations, in Christian work and in local churches. Church hoppers—and self-proclaimed spiritual vigilantes—are on the increase.

I recently heard about a church that experienced a tremendous amount of growth in its inception. A seven thousand-seat auditorium was built to handle the continuous influx of new members. Everything was going great. But now, within a relatively short amount of time, that building sits there with many empty pews. Why did this happen? Because the leadership of the church was accused of several mistakes, which no one could actually prove. However, in the end, most of the members left overnight.

When you are active in a local body of believers, when you support your local church and pastor, when you pray for Christian ministries, you will soon find that there will be problems. But don't pack your bags and walk off. Don't forsake your friendships.

If you are a true friend to someone, you will not abandon them when they have problems—you will stay with them and pray with them. We need to develop this character in our churches, our prayer fellowships and in our ministries so our brothers and sisters will not suffer needlessly.

There is a saying I have heard: "You don't burn the barn down just to kill a rat." If you have a barn, you expect to find a few rats—it's normal. But you don't demolish the place just to kill them. You look for the rats!

When you face a problem that looms large in your vision, keep these two things in mind: First of all, pray about it. Commit yourself to pray for your leaders, for the ministries you know, for the church, for the pastor and for those people who are stirring up the problems.

Then focus your heart on the other 99 percent good that is happening. Determine that you will see the problem for what it really is—in light of everything else, not standing by itself.

Let us purpose to see the problems that we deal with in the total picture of what God is doing. And even when we are faced with injustices, even when our rights are violated, let us say with Paul, "What then? notwithstanding, every way ... Christ is preached; and I therein do rejoice, yea, and will rejoice" (Phil. 1:18).

Well, He Did It—So I Can Too

The second attack Satan will wage against followers of Jesus is *the temptation to become self-centered by rationalization.* "Everybody's doing it, so it must be okay," we reason. "I will too." This is what some call the herd instinct mentality.

I heard a story on the radio recently. A man was driving in his car and came to a huge bridge. He saw another man standing rather close to the edge, looking down into the river. The thought occurred to the driver of the car that this guy may be about to commit suicide.

He stopped his car and went over to the man, hoping to counsel him to save his life. In the end, both men jumped off the bridge to their deaths.

To me this is a perfect illustration of human nature. You see, our flesh never looks for what it can do for God's kingdom. Rather, it is always searching for what it can get for itself. As a result, we are easily swayed to become self-centered. All we have to do is rationalize a bit.

There is an interesting event in John 21, which takes place after Jesus was resurrected, when Peter decided to go back to fishing once again.

"Simon Peter saith unto them, I go a fishing. They [the disciples] say unto him, We also go with thee" (John 21:3).

What did these other disciples say? "Well, Peter, if you are going, then we are going too." They were easily influenced by Peter's decision; we aren't much different.

It is so easy to rationalize our actions, our decisions and our thoughts. It can happen to anyone.

When your heart becomes discouraged, when doubts rise in your mind, when you are tired and want out of the battle, remember this: It doesn't matter what happens to anyone else. Your only concern is to follow the Lord.

Peter was used by Satan to pull the disciples away from their commitment to Jesus and run after the fishing nets and boats again. I pray that none of us will become an instrument in the hand of the enemy to cause another brother or sister to stumble.

When William Carey heard the call of the Lord to go to India, he shared the tremendous burden on his heart with the elders in his congregation. Their response was, "Sit down, young man. If God wants to save those heathens, He'll find someone else." Carey had no friends. He had to make the decision to obey the Lord's calling alone.

What about Daniel and his friends? They stood alone, captives in a foreign land. They chose to follow God's law and faced isolation, persecution and even the loss of their lives.

What about Enoch? Genesis 5 records a long list of names, and in the middle of the list we read, "And Enoch walked with God." All alone, it seems.

Jeremiah faced four decades of prophecy, lamenting, rejection, misunderstandings and persecution—and had to stand all alone.

We know Jesus had to face the same thing. And to His disciples Jesus said, "I am sending you out as sheep among wolves" (see Luke 10:3).

We must not look for approval from everybody as we seek to build the Lord's kingdom. Sometimes you must set your face against the cold wind and walk all alone.

The enemy will use many voices around you to attack you so that you begin to question your calling. You rationalize what you hear and say, "Well, what can I do? My father is against me, my mother is against me, my brothers and sisters, the whole congregation, everyone is against me—so I guess the Lord isn't calling me after all. I'd better not go."

When Moses sent the spies out to Canaan, the majority of the group was against going into the land. Only Joshua and Caleb said, "We can go and win," but no one would listen to them because they were the minority. People even picked up stones to stone them.

The enemy uses many voices to distract us from our calling. But, remember, Jesus told us our life with Him would lead down a narrow road. Be watchful and alert so that you aren't deceived by the majority.

We must never forget what Jesus said: "He that loveth father or mother more than me is not worthy of me: and he that loveth son or daughter more than me is not worthy of me" (Matt. 10:37).

And don't forget that Jesus' own brothers came to snatch him away, saying that He had mental problems (see Mark 3:21, John 7:5).

In following Christ, our closest relatives—even parents—can be against us. Jesus said, "Think not that I am come to send peace on earth: I came not to send peace, but a sword. For I am come to set a man at variance against his father, and the daughter against her mother, and the daughter in law against her mother in law. And a man's foes shall be they of his own household" (Matt. 10:34-36). But we are called to keep our allegiance to God's revealed Word, to obey Him and follow Him.

This is true even today in the Muslim and Hindu communities. Many young people who come to the Lord refuse to bow down before idols in the temples or worship in the mosque, and for this they are killed. They are willing to take a stand against the deeply entrenched family system.

You also must know the call of Christ beyond the

shadow of a doubt if you are to commit radically to Him, abandoning your life.

Don't let the majority become the tool of the enemy to deceive you. That doesn't mean we shouldn't listen to the wisdom of those in our prayer fellowship or congregation. The Bible tells us that "Where no counsel is, the people fall: but in the multitude of counsellors there is safety" (Prov. 11:14). There is a balance to all of this. But this is one of the areas where we need to be extremely watchful of the enemy's tactics.

Watching for Fiery Darts

The third way the enemy attacks us is by *causing us to forget that we do have an enemy*. Satan's desire is not to withhold funds or stop plans from being carried out. His plan is to make us as believers ineffective in the work of the kingdom.

You see, God is never troubled by the lack of money, ideas or plans. His greatest purpose is to find people. "For the eyes of the Lord run to and fro throughout the whole earth, to shew himself strong in the behalf of them whose heart is perfect toward him" (2 Chron. 16:9).

It is individuals—you and I—whom God has chosen to change the course of this generation. Sometimes we forget this—but Satan has never forgotten it. As servants of the Lord, we are an awesome threat to the enemy. He does his best to make us as ineffective as possible for the Lord.

As followers of Jesus in a fallen world, we are not immune to the devil's attacks. His fiery darts are constantly thrown at us. We face discouragement, sorrows, misunderstandings and disappointments. The tiniest thing can be used by Satan to waste the precious time we have been given.

We need to realize how important it is to pray for God's protection over one another. No one is exempt from these struggles—especially those of us who are serving the Lord on the front lines.

We have no need to be afraid of the enemy's schemes—we are told to "resist the devil, and he will flee from you" (James 4:7). John encourages us, "Ye are of God, little children, and have overcome them: because greater is he that is in you, than he that is in the world" (1 John 4:4).

Paul tells us to stand firm and pray always (Eph. 6:13,18). Unless we stay in the battle, we can easily get crushed by the enemy.

Let me share some encouraging words that came across my desk recently.

"The Lord has given every man his work. It is his business to do it, and the devil's business to hinder him if he can. And as sure as God has given you a work to do, Satan will try to hinder you.

"My dear Christian friend, *KEEP AT YOUR WORK*. Do not flinch because the lion roars; do not stop to stone the devil's dogs; do not fool away your time chasing the devil's rabbits. Do your work. Let liars lie, let religious sectarians quarrel, let corporations resolve, the editors publish, and come what may, let the devil do his worst; but see to it that *nothing* hinders you from fulfilling the work God has given you.

"Keep at your work. Let your aim be as steady as a star. Let the world brawl and babble and bubble. Keep at your work. You may be assaulted, wronged, insulted, slandered, wounded and rejected; you may be abused by foes, forsaken by friends and despised and rejected of men, but see to it with steadfast determination, with unfaltering zeal, that you pursue the great purpose of your life and the object of your

being, until at last you can say, "I have run the race …
I have finished the work which Thou gavest me to do."
(Author Unknown)

The Victory That Overcomes the World

Finally, one of the strongest attacks of the enemy
against believers is to *cause us to forget the need to
exercise our faith in God.* Hebrews 11:6 says,
"Without faith it is impossible to please him."

There are times in our lives when we have more
questions than answers. Our emotions are dry and cold.
Nothing gives us reason to get excited or happy about
serving God.

What do we do? Times like these are part of the
battle. This is when "the just shall live by his faith"
(Hab. 2:4). In every battle we face, we need to keep in
mind that faith is the key that helps us to overcome the
world and the enemy. "And this is the victory that
overcometh the world, even our faith" (1 John 5:4).

After spying out the land of Canaan, Joshua and
Caleb said, "Let's go!" Caleb especially was a radical
revolutionary type. He told Moses and the people of
Israel, "Let us go up at once, and possess it; for we are
well able to overcome it" (Num. 13:30).

But what did the other ten spies say? "Oh, no, this
is impossible! We can't do this—we saw giants in the
land, and we saw ourselves as grasshoppers compared
to them" (see Num. 13:33).

Forty-five years later, when it was time for Israel
to finally enter the land of Canaan, Caleb, at age
eighty-five, was still ready to go and possess his
inheritance. "I am as strong this day as I was in the day
that Moses sent me: as my strength was then, even so
is my strength now, for war, both to go out, and to
come in.

"Now therefore give me this mountain, whereof

the LORD spake in that day ... if so be the LORD will be with me, then I shall be able to drive them out, as the LORD said" (Josh. 14:12).

Caleb lived his whole life following the Lord. When he saw the land of Canaan, he had no doubt that the children of Israel could possess it, because he was confident in God's ability to go beyond any weakness or frailty.

God honored Caleb's faith and gave him his own inheritance in the promised land, because, as Moses told him, "thou hast wholly followed the LORD my God" (Josh. 14:9).

If you know anything about faith, you also know that there is something innate within us human beings that always works *against* faith. Even within the most knowledgeable theologian, the most powerful preacher, there is always something that naturally works against faith. "But the natural man receiveth not the things of the Spirit of God: for they are foolishness unto him" (1 Cor. 2:14).

No matter how much we read and memorize the Bible, our natural mind always comes up with some argument against God's way of doing things. This is why exercising faith is so very important.

The Lord makes a clear distinction in Isaiah 55:7-9 between His thoughts and those of man.

"Let the wicked forsake his way, and the unrighteous man *his thoughts:* and let him return unto the LORD, and he will have mercy upon him; and to our God, for he will abundantly pardon.

"For my thoughts are not your thoughts, neither are your ways my ways, saith the LORD. For as the heavens are higher than the earth, so are my ways higher than your ways, and my thoughts than your thoughts."

Paul exhorted the believers in Corinth—and us

today as well—that an important part of spiritual warfare involves dealing with our natural thoughts, those that work against faith.

"For though we walk in the flesh, we do not war after the flesh: (For the weapons of our warfare are not carnal, but mighty through God to the pulling down of strong holds;) *casting down imaginations*, and every high thing that exalteth itself against the knowledge of God, and *bringing into captivity every thought* to the obedience of Christ" (2 Cor. 10:3-5).

When Elisha the prophet was serving the Lord in Israel, a very powerful Syrian captain called Naaman came to him. He had heard that Elisha could heal him of his leprosy. Elisha made a very strange request of him: "Go and wash in Jordan seven times, and thy flesh shall come again to thee, and thou shalt be clean" (2 Kings 5:10).

Naaman became very angry when he heard this. After all, he wasn't a small man in the kingdom of Syria—and what the prophet asked him to do was ridiculous! Naaman was outraged. The word in the King James is *wroth,* and it translates to mean that he burst out in anger. The man probably spewed out a stream of vulgarities at the top of his lungs.

And why was he so angry? Verse 11 records Naaman's explanation: "Behold, I *thought*, He will surely come out to me, and stand, and call on the name of the LORD his God, and strike his hand over the place, and recover the leper."

No matter what God says, our own thoughts will somehow either try to get the job done, or say it can't be done, it isn't God's will for it to be done, or that it isn't the way He works. Our mind will always come up with something to counteract what God asks us to do.

What can we do about our wayward mind? First of all, we must search our hearts and make sure there is nothing that keeps us from uniting our hearts with one another. The Bible tells us that *if two shall agree on anything, it shall be done* (see Matt. 18:19).

The other important thing to keep in mind is what Jesus told us in Mark 11:24: "Therefore I say unto you, What things soever ye desire, when ye pray, *believe that ye receive them,* and ye shall have them." So many have used this verse out of context over the years that we have a tendency to write it off. You know what? It's in your Bible and mine as well!

When you pray for an unsaved loved one, when you pray for a revival in your church, when you pray for a spiritual breakthrough in Islamic countries, when you pray that the unsaved will be reached with the gospel, remember what Jesus said: "Believe that you have received it."

When God told Abraham he would have a son, Abraham not only believed it but he also began to thank God. Later on, he received his son.

I encourage you to exercise your faith actively in what God is able to do. Go beyond your natural thoughts and reactions. In obedience to what the Word of God says, trust Him for miracles far greater than what your mind could imagine.

Not Just a Regular Job

I agree that there is no point in investing our time and energy to study the devil's work and his intricate strategies. Yet, for those of us who serve the Lord and are committed to His purposes, I want to stress how important it is to be aware, to be sensitive. We are a major threat to the powers of darkness.

It is vitally important for us to remember that our walk and our service to the Lord is not a normal, nine-to-five, five-day-a-week job where we clock in and clock out. By the very nature of the fact that you have committed yourself to the Lord, you must realize that you will face problems. You will face attacks.

Therefore, our safeguard is to be aware of these things daily. And as we take up the weapons of our warfare as described in Ephesians 6, we will be overcomers in this battle. "Wherefore take unto you the whole armour of God, that ye may be able to withstand in the evil day, and having done all, to stand" (Eph. 6:13).

Living in the Light of Eternity

Chapter 6

BRINGING OUR HEARTS
BACK INTO FOCUS

O n the way back from India, I usually have at least eight or ten hours of layover in Bombay before catching my flight back to the States. One fellow worker, whom I know from my Operation Mobilization days, opens his home to me for a few hours of rest, for which I am always grateful.

On one particular occasion the entire family was gone, and I was alone in the house. They had given me a room with a bed, and I was glad for some quiet. My schedule had been rather heavy on this last trip. So many wonderful things were happening on the mission field, which gave me many reasons to praise the Lord, but it also meant more expended energy on my part.

As I lay there, my pent-up feelings of frustration and weariness swept over me. *Why am I doing this?* I asked myself. *What is it all about anyway?*

As I poured out my heart to the Lord, I knew the answer to my questions. I said out loud, "The only reason I should even live is to win those who do not know Jesus. If I don't do this, there is really no reason for me to live. Absolutely not."

Nothing gives purpose to my life except doing the will of the Father and winning souls for Christ. Nothing else is really permanent. Someday everything on this earth will be gone.

Why Am I Doing This?

Recently I met with a couple who talked with me about their calling as missionaries to France. After sharing in churches for two years, they still had not been able to raise even 70 percent of their needed income. Most churches put their own agenda— whether it is buildings, staff or special programs—as first priority in their budgets. Missions are somewhere on down the list.

As believers we must constantly be alert to the ever-present danger of losing that fine focus of our true purpose in this life. Somehow the pressures of this life, our immediate needs and our current struggles come to the forefront of our thinking. We so easily fall into the trap of becoming just like anybody else. Our little headache becomes more serious than ethnic cleansing in Europe or an earthquake in China.

We must continually bring our lives and our hearts back into focus. We must each ask ourselves, *Why am I doing this? Why am I giving my life to serve the Lord?*

We face struggles on all sides. How do we remain full of joy and spiritually on the move?

As followers of Jesus, our purpose in life is radically different from that of the rest of the world. It is not to build an organization, to attain financial security or to be remembered for noble deeds.

What really matters is this: Keeping our eyes, our hearts and our actions focused on reaching this generation with the gospel. According to what Jesus said in the Great Commission, this is our number one priority.

The Bottom Line

During the last year or so I've been able to talk about my burden for world evangelism in several television roundtable discussions. It's been interesting for me to meet with others who share similar and differing viewpoints.

In one recent show our discussion became quite involved over the issue of "scaling down," or living with less. Suddenly I realized our conversation had taken a philosophical turn, and we were offering very little practical application to the topic.

"My goodness," I said to the rest of the group, "what does all this mean to the people who are watching the program? We are sitting here debating over policies and philosophies while millions are plunging into hell.

"The Christians who are watching this program need to understand one thing about scaling down their life-styles: One hundred years from now—what will remain? Their houses, their money, their plans, their buildings—nothing will have meaning any longer. It will be gone. It will all be over.

"We must sell out now and invest our lives to reach the lost world. We must adjust our life-styles in the light of hell."

This is the bottom line. Our purpose in life does not consist of going to school, graduating, finding a job, getting married, having children, sending them to school and so on. If we see only that part of life, we will continually be bogged down with the battle of our own personal problems. We need to see beyond all that.

In the last chapter I mentioned how William Carey had to stand alone against the tide of opinion held by the elders of his church. His wife, Dorothy, also resisted his decision. Although Carey felt strongly called to go to India, Dorothy refused to go with him. He knew he could not disobey the call of God on his life, and so he chose to go on, even if she would not. The ship pulled away from the dock and sailed away, leaving her behind.

Then something on board broke down, and the ship had to return to the port for repairs. During the delay, Dorothy reconsidered and chose to go to India with her husband. Later she lost all ability to cope in India and suffered a mental breakdown. Carey was left to care for the children alone.

William Carey spent many years in India serving his Lord, and they were not easy ones. He paid an extremely high price to follow Jesus. His list of personal problems went on and on—but he saw beyond the pain and agony and remembered the purpose of his life.

Remembering That Lives Are at Stake

Ultimately, two major forces impact what happens on earth: the living God and the powers of darkness—Satan and his demons.

Satan has only one goal in mind: to take as many people into hell as possible.

The Lord, through His mercy, is seeking to bring as many people to repentance as possible, so they might know Him and reign with Him forever.

One of the strongest and most successful attacks of

the enemy on the work of God is to cause us to forget our purpose and our goal. We find ourselves so wrapped up in who we are and what we are doing that we are no longer able to answer those questions, *Why am I here? And what am I living for?*

Why are we here on this earth? What is the purpose behind our lives? It is the multiplied millions of people, over two billion of them in fact, who have not yet been reached with the gospel and are on their way to hell. These are people just like you and me—they are not rats or snakes or monkeys. They are human beings, just as precious in the sight of God as you and I.

If you were inside your home and suddenly heard someone outside yelling, "Your house is on fire—get out, get out!" what would you do? Would you stand there and talk it over with your family? No! You would break a door through the wall if you had to! You would find any way possible to get out. It would be too risky, too dangerous to stay there any longer.

The situation around us is much worse than a house on fire. People's souls are at stake, and we have an opportunity to do something about it. We have an opportunity to take millions with us to heaven instead of allowing them to die in their sins.

But how can we so comfortably live for ourselves while millions slip into an eternal hell? We can do it because the enemy has managed to replace our focus on eternity with a desire for comfort and self-realization.

A Lifesaving Station

Let me share with you a modern-day parable that sheds some light on the condition of the church today.

"On a dangerous seacoast where shipwrecks often

occurred, there was once a crude little lifesaving station. The building was just a hut, and there was only one boat; but the few devoted members kept a constant watch over the sea. And with no thought for themselves, they went out day and night, tirelessly searching for the lost.

"Some of those who were saved and various others in the surrounding area wanted to become associated with the station and give of their time and money and effort for the support of its work. New boats were bought, and new crews were trained. The little lifesaving station grew.

"Some of the members of the lifesaving station were unhappy that the building was so crude and poorly equipped. They felt that a more comfortable place should be provided as the first refuge for those saved from the sea. They replaced the emergency cots with beds and put better furniture in the enlarged building.

"The lifesaving station became a popular gathering place for its members, and they decorated it beautifully and furnished it exquisitely, because they used it as a sort of club. Fewer members were now interested in going out to sea on lifesaving missions, and so they hired lifeboat crews to do the work. The lifesaving motif still prevailed in the club's decorations: There was a liturgical lifeboat in the room where the club initiations were held.

"About this time a large ship was wrecked off the coast, and the hired crews brought in boatloads of cold, wet and half-drowned people. They were dirty and sick, and some of them had black skin, and some of them had yellow skin. The beautiful new club was in chaos. So the property committee immediately had a shower built outside the club, where the victims of the shipwreck could be cleaned up before coming inside.

"After the next meeting, there was a split in the club membership. Most of the members wanted to stop the club's lifesaving activities because they were unpleasant and a hindrance to the normal social life of the club. Some members insisted on lifesaving as their primary purpose and pointed out that they were still called a lifesaving station. But they were finally voted down and told that if they wanted to save lives of all various kinds of people who were shipwrecked in those waters, they could begin their own lifesaving station down the coast. They did.

"As the years went by, the new station experienced the same changes that occurred in the old. It evolved into a club, and yet another lifesaving station was founded.

"History continued to repeat itself, and if you visit that seacoast today, you will find a number of exclusive clubs along the shore. Shipwrecks are frequent in those waters, but most of the people drown."

Thinking in Terms of Ourselves

Our tendency as horizontally oriented humans is to view our lives as such. We see, we hear, we smell, we touch, we taste. The temptation is to forget the war that is going on behind the scenes and to interpret everything in our lives through the filter of our five senses.

All of a sudden we are thinking in terms of ourselves rather than the purpose the Lord has given us as believers. Now anything that has to do with our senses is our first approach to solving problems and dilemmas. The personal problems we face suddenly take precedence over everything else. Circumstances dictate how we feel and what we do.

We have lost our focus, and this is exactly what the enemy wants.

We are not made for time. We are created for eternity. Our life right now is simply a little classroom in which we are learning to be conformed to the image of the Lord Jesus Christ (Rom. 8:29).

And what was the purpose of Christ's life? Why did He come into this world? What did He live for? "To seek and to save that which was lost" (Luke 19:10). And the more we become like Christ, the more we too will make world evangelism top priority in our lives.

Do you see how everything else in life becomes so incidental when we gain this focus? Our clothes, our food, our hairstyles, our makeup, our bank accounts, our education, our degrees, our plans and ambition, our children, our spouses—all these things cannot be the most important things in life.

During World War II, the people of England scaled down their life-styles to the barest of essentials. They knew that if they didn't fully commit themselves to winning the war, they would lose everything. They gladly gave their money, their gold, their silver and even their children. The people of England remembered the war.

A Man Who Remembered

Shankar, a native missionary in North India, was born in a leper colony to parents who were themselves stricken with leprosy. In order to save Shankar from contracting the disease, Brother Thomas, one of our native missionary leaders, raised him in a home he had built for children of lepers.

Shankar received a good education, and with it a chance to make a better life for himself.

During his time with Brother Thomas, Shankar

gave his life to the Lord and received a call to full-time ministry. Just before Shankar's graduation from Bible school, Brother Thomas told him he was free to go to a pioneer area and begin mission work there.

"No," Shankar replied, "I will work among my own people—the lepers—and tell them how the Lord has changed my life. I will tell them how He can save them."

Today Shankar has laid down everything he has gained—his education and his chance for a better life—to live and work as a missionary in the leper colonies of India.

Shankar did not lose the focus. He remembered his purpose as a follower of Jesus.

Just a Bunch of Sheep

Not too long ago I came away from a conversation with one of our leaders in India feeling disturbed and upset. Five years before, a young man had joined our headquarters staff in India. He was excited about the work and was intensely committed to the ministry.

Over the last six months, however, I had seen signs of deterioration in his commitment. I warned our leaders, "You need to talk to this brother. Something is missing."

Then I received a phone call telling me this brother had found an opportunity to make more money in one of the Gulf countries, and so he decided to leave. Just like that. I was disappointed in his decision to leave and in the evident change in his heart.

But, you see, it didn't happen overnight. It was a gradual process that finally revealed itself in his decision to leave the ministry so he could make more money.

Throughout the Bible we humans are compared to

sheep. Do you know what one of the predominant characteristics of sheep is? They stray quite a bit.

Built-in Breakdown

If we do not diligently watch over our hearts, we will soon be off track. It may take months or even years, but eventually our actions will follow the direction our heart has led. We will find every reason under the sun to justify our actions and our choices. Finally, we are completely out of the battle. We are no longer serving or even following the Lord.

They say that when cars are manufactured, they are designed with a built-in obsolescence factor. In other words, the car is made to run well for a few years, and then after a time it will begin to break down and become obsolete. The consumer is expected to return to the dealership after a few years and begin the entire process all over again.

In the human heart there is a built-in obsolescence factor as well. It doesn't matter who you are, how powerful and influential you are, how much education you have, how self-controlled or holy you consider yourself—your heart will break down and stray away from the Lord *if you do not guard it.*

I have too often seen this principle played out in the church at large as well as in individual's lives. Unfortunately, many churches today have drifted away from the heart of the One they call Lord and Master.

Now, instead of making it a priority to rescue the lost millions of the world from a Christless eternity, their programs revolve around themselves.

Proverbs 24:11-12 warns us, "If thou forbear [neglect] to deliver them that are drawn unto death, and those that are ready to be slain; if thou sayest, Behold, we knew it not; doth not he that pondereth the heart consider it? and he that keepeth thy soul, doth not he know it? and shall not he render to every man according to his works?"

Not too long ago I traveled to speak in a church which was involved in missions to a limited extent.

After the meeting I went to get a bite to eat with the couple who had been our contact for this meeting. Our conversation lasted well into the night.

"You know, Brother K.P.," the husband told me, "I never really understood what is happening in the church with regard to missions until I read your books.

"Our church offers solid, Bible-based teaching. In fact, it is one of the best Bible-teaching churches in the entire region. But with all this knowledge, I am sad to tell you that we are spending more money on our own social programs than on missions!"

I do not want to make a big case out of this—I simply want to illustrate my point. Not all churches are like this one. I do not desire to pass judgment on anyone, much less the church at large. But I want to ask one question: Is the church so back-slidden, so far gone from the reality of what is happening outside its four walls, that it is impossible to revive?

The Cry of the Blood

Amy Carmichael, one of the great pioneer missionaries to India, wrote a little tract called *Thy Brother's Blood Crieth*. This is what she wrote about what happened one night as she lay in her bed:

"The tom-toms thumped straight on all night, and the darkness shuddered round me like a living, feeling thing. I could not go to sleep, so I lay awake and looked; and I saw, as it seemed, this:

"That I stood on a grassy sward, and at my feet a precipice broke sheer down into infinite space. I looked, but saw no bottom; only cloud shapes, black and furiously coiled, and great shadow-shrouded hollows, and unfathomable depths. Back I drew, dizzy at the depth.

"Then I saw forms of people moving single file along the grass. They were making for the edge. There was a woman with a baby in her arms and another little child holding onto her dress. She was on the very verge. Then I saw that she was blind. She lifted her foot for the next step...it trod air. She was over, and the children over with her. Oh, the cry as they went over!

"Then I saw more streams of people flowing from all quarters. All were blind, stone blind; all made straight for the precipice edge. There were shrieks as they suddenly knew themselves falling, and a tossing up of helpless arms, catching, clutching at empty air. But some went over quietly, and fell without a sound.

"Then I wondered, with a wonder that was simply agony, why no one stopped them at the edge. I could not. I was glued to the ground, and I could not call; though I strained and tried, only a whisper would come.

"Then I saw that along the edge there were sentries set at intervals. But the intervals were too great; there were wide, unguarded gaps between. And over these gaps the people fell in their blindness, quite unwarned; and the green grass seemed blood-red to me, and the gulf yawned like the mouth of hell.

"Then I saw, like a little picture of peace, a group of people under some trees with their backs turned towards the gulf. They were making daisy chains. Sometimes when a piercing shriek cut the quiet air and reached them, it disturbed them and they thought it a rather vulgar noise. And if one of their number started up and wanted to go and do something to help, then all the others would pull that one down. 'Why should you get so excited about it? You must wait for a definite call to go! You haven't finished your daisy chain yet. It would be really selfish,' they said, 'to leave us to finish the work alone.'

"There was another group. It was made up of people whose great desire was to get more sentries out; but they found that very few wanted to go, and sometimes there were no sentries set for miles and miles of the edge.

"Once a girl stood alone in her place, waving the people back; but her mother and other relations called, and reminded her that her furlough was due; she must not break the rules. And being tired and needing a change, she had to go and rest for awhile; but no one was sent to guard her gap, and over and over the people fell, like a waterfall of souls.

"Once a child caught at a tuft of grass that grew at the very brink of the gulf; it clung convulsively, and it called—but nobody seemed to hear. Then the roots of the grass gave way, and with a cry the child went over, its two little hands still holding tight to the torn-off bunch of grass. And the girl who longed to be back in her gap thought she heard the little one cry, and she sprang up and wanted to go; at which they reproved her, reminding her that no one is necessary anywhere; the gap would be well taken care of, they knew. And then they sang a hymn.

"Then through the hymn came another sound like the pain of a million broken hearts wrung out in one full drop, one sob. And a horror of great darkness was upon me, for I knew what it was—the Cry of the Blood.

"Then thundered a voice, the voice of the Lord. 'And He said, "What hast thou done? The voice of thy brother's blood crieth unto me from the ground."'

"The tom-toms still beat heavily, the darkness still shuddered and shivered about me....

"What does it matter, after all? It has gone on for years; it will go on for years. Why make such a fuss about it?

"God forgive us! God arouse us! Shame us out of our callousness! Shame us out of our sin!"[1]

I have been told that when this tract was printed and circulated in the West, many in the church criticized Amy Carmichael for putting out a tract like this, telling her that she was condemning them as though they were the worst of heathens.

We must remember this: Unless we think carefully, unless we make deliberate decisions, we will walk in the way of all flesh.

In the next chapter we'll take a heartbreaking glimpse of those multitudes who are plunging over the cliff.

Chapter 7

LIVING WITH THE REALITY

In the past three to five years the world has experienced events that no one would have even dared to dream about. We have stood by in amazement while whole countries reshaped practically overnight, world systems crumbled into the pages of history books, and political maps changed faster than cartographers could redraw them.

For all this to happen, there must have been a tremendous confrontation of spiritual forces in the unseen world. We can clearly see the effects of it on the cutting edge of missions. The hand of God is moving in an unprecedented way. There is a hunger for the living God that we did not see even ten or twenty years ago. The harvest is ripe.

We may not understand all that is taking place in

the spiritual realm, but this one thing is clear: The coming of Jesus is very, very near.

Right now the possibility to reach our generation with the gospel of Jesus Christ is better than at any other time in history. The opportunities are unlimited, and the church has the resources.

But what I see happening in Christian circles concerns me deeply. Believers are being bombarded from all sides to invest their time, their efforts and their finances into everything but a lost and dying world. The material things they must buy, the trips, the social gatherings, the building projects, the comfort of their families—all of these are at the expense of souls who are lost for eternity.

Those believers who have already committed their lives to reaching the world with the gospel are in danger of losing sight of the big picture. When emotions are down, when times are difficult, it's easy to focus on self and desire to get out of the battle.

The key to both of these problems is to keep the reality of the lost world before our eyes. Then our needs, our wants, our struggles and our discouragements will no longer be a priority.

What Shocks and Moves Me?

During the heat of the Gulf War, I was as glued to the news as anyone. I kept my radio on as much as possible, straining for any new piece of information. Usually I spend my early-morning hours preparing my radio broadcasts; but during the war I had a hard time concentrating. I wanted to know what was going on!

As believers committed to reaching the lost, you and I are given more information about what is going on in the world today than ever before. We know more about the Muslims, the Hindus, the Buddhists and ethnic groups than the generations of believers who went before us.

But let me ask you this question: How seriously do you really take this information?

You see, the war that we deal with on a daily basis—the battle that rages for souls of men and women like you and me—is infinitely more serious than any war on this earth.

When a Scud missile hit a military barracks during the war, killing twenty-eight soldiers and wounding hundreds, the whole American nation was shaken by the news. It shocked and moved the White House. The media could talk of nothing else.

But does it move us to think that *eighty thousand people are slipping into hell every twenty-four hours?*

I remember hearing about a particular victory won by the anti-Iraqi forces. After hearing the details, I walked calmly back to my desk to resume my studies. Suddenly the conviction of the Lord came upon me so strongly that I had to sit down. The reality of what I had actually heard hit me with full force. It was more than jet fighters and a few missiles. It was the fate of thousands of Muslims—and now I saw them as the Lord did, desperately lost and headed for hell.

"Is it nothing to you that these people are dying and going to hell?" the Lord asked me.

There are over one billion Muslims living in the world today who do not know the love of Christ. I didn't even think about the eternal implications of the news I'd heard.

I didn't even spend one minute to stop and pray for these people, that they would have a chance to come to the Lord. I casually heard the news and then went about my business.

As the Lord spoke strongly to my heart that day, I could only sit there and repent of my attitude.

Familiarity Breeds ...

Somewhere along the way we have become so familiar with the information we are given that our hearts become hardened and cold.

But the questions remain: Are there tears in our eyes for the lost and dying millions? When we hear news about the world around us, do our hearts break for those who are going to hell? Is getting up in the morning to spend time with the Lord and pray for the lost becoming a burden?

We all need to have our hearts continually broken before the Lord. You see, in the normal course of human nature, things never improve. Unless we allow the Holy Spirit to continually renew our hearts and our minds, deterioration, coldness and bitterness will set in. We will take the things of the Lord casually. We will find all sorts of rational excuses to prove why our thinking is correct, and why we should justify ourselves.

Restoring Us to Tenderheartedness

There are so many needs and opportunities on the mission field. Please don't let your involvement stop at: "Well, I'm doing the best I can." Is your heart still beating with the same tenderness and passion for the dying world? Is your sensitivity still fresh?

I have to continually come before the Lord and ask, "Lord, am I getting too used to it all? Is everything so familiar to me? Do I simply get up before congregations and say the same things over and over again? Is my passion an automatic thing—or is my heart fresh and new?"

I remember the time, somewhere in the late '70s, when I first met David Mains, director of The Chapel of the Air. I had never seen the man before. All I knew was that he had a radio program, and I hoped that he as a Christian leader would hear my story. There I was, sitting in his office, wearing my wedding suit and a beat-up tie.

He graciously gave me his time and allowed me to share with him my vision for supporting native missionaries. I will never forget sitting there, talking for an hour and a half with him, and weeping as I shared the needs of the brothers on the mission field.

When I remember those days, I ask myself, *Do I still weep for the lost? Is that burden and vision still fresh in my heart?*

As followers of Jesus, the things we do—whether we are praying, giving, sending or going ourselves— will greatly determine what happens on the other side of the world. I encourage you to search your heart. Is the passion still there? Is your heart broken?

You see, when we lose that tenderness, it's like putting sand in the gears of a machine. They will still crank, but you must work so much harder for anything to happen, and the grinding noise is constant and grating.

No one can restore that freshness, that passion, for you. You must come before the Lord and allow Him to renew your heart.

Seeing the Big Picture

Apart from the things of the Lord, there are two things we value most in our lives: 1) we want to feel important, and 2) we want to be a part of something important. No one wants to feel as though they're wasting their lives away.

When we are involved in any work for the Lord, at times it becomes difficult to keep sight of how our investment in His kingdom is making a difference. Satan can use those busy times in our lives to breed discouragement and bitterness and render us ineffective in the work of the Lord.

We need to see the big picture of what the Lord is doing so that the enemy will not use our immediate struggles, frustrations, disappointments or demands on our time to cause us to become discouraged.

The immediate in our lives always takes precedence over everything else.

Ask the Lord, and then allow Him to give you glimpses *beyond* the immediate to the lives of those people you are impacting through your obedience and service to Him.

Looking Beyond Our Individual Lives

The other day I made a phone call to the pastor of a church where I spoke recently. I was encouraged to hear of some of the results of my being there.

"Brother K.P.," the pastor said, "it all began with your coming to our church. Ever since you came here, we are baptizing people every Sunday. Our people are no longer the same. They still talk about what the Lord has done in their hearts. One of the key men in the church has just finished reading *The Road to Reality*. There are incredible changes taking place in his life!"

He went on for several minutes, saying he had never seen such growth in the lives of the people before.

I am grateful that the Lord could do this through me. But do you think this happened just because I left India one day and decided to come speak in this church? No. It was a process, involving many years and many people. I was simply reaping where I did not bestow any labor (see John 4:38).

Let us not become sidetracked, our vision fogged, where we can see only the immediate situation and nothing beyond. We must look beyond our individual lives, and it takes grace and maturity to do so.

The body of Christ today reminds me of an elephant. Did you know that the elephant is the only one who doesn't know how big his body is? His eyes are too small, and he has two huge ears sticking out right beside them! So he walks around like a little animal, led by a small boy with a stick.

We aren't able to see all that results from our efforts for the Lord, but we can be encouraged, knowing by faith that God in His mercy is able to use His body to make an incredible impact on the world.

Let me encourage you to pursue what the Lord has given you to do. What you are doing is more than just "work." I plead with you to remember that life on earth, no matter where you are, has its struggles, its conflicts, its discouragements.

Joseph had done nothing wrong and walked in total purity and commitment. He was obedient to his parents and his brothers. What did he do wrong to be sold into slavery and thrown into prison for thirteen years? What did he do wrong to lose everything he called his own? No reason is given in the Bible. Those thirteen years were crucial, though, for him to be able to reign as prime minister over Egypt.

No Price Is Too High

Recently I received two very special letters. Terry and Jane, with their children John and Sara, had been supporting several native missionaries through Gospel for Asia as a family. Now John and Sara wanted to support one individually as well.

"My Mom and Dad support some missionaries, so

my sister and I decided to support a missionary," wrote John.

Sara added, "I am glad you have started this work. Please send us a missionary to pray for and support."

I was so blessed and encouraged to read their letters and to know that these children are already beginning to invest their lives in eternity.

In my mind's eye, I look forward to that day when we will all see Jesus face to face. As believers from all times and places are united before His throne, we will offer Him the praise He is worthy to receive.

John and Sara will be there. So will their mom and dad, and multitudes of others who laid down their lives for the sake of the kingdom, whether by praying and sending others or by going themselves.

As we worship our Lord, others will also join us— men and women from every tongue and tribe and nation, those for whom others prayed and gave and lived and even died. As we gather around His throne, we will know beyond any doubt that no price was too high to pay to serve Jesus. It was worth it all.

Keeping the Reality Before Our Eyes

When was the last time you wept because your heart was burdened for those dying without ever hearing the name of Jesus? When was the last time you spent an evening praying over a world map?

Let us not lose our motivation and leave the battle because we are not willing to live with the reality that half the world is still waiting to hear the gospel.

The cry of the lost world comes loud and desperate to our ears. Let us be willing to hear it and respond to it. Let us allow the Lord to break our hearts for the lost. He is willing—and waiting—to do some major things through us, but our hearts must be soft and tender first.

God is bigger than all we are, or all we want to be. He is in the process of making us into His image. See the big picture—go beyond the limits of your own narrow perspective and allow the Lord to use your life for eternity.

If we keep this reality before our eyes, we can no longer live for ourselves—our needs and desires, our struggles and disappointments. Instead, we will give up our own ambitions to make sacrifices—laying down our very lives so that others will know Jesus. In this final hour let us choose the cross and not turn back.

Living in the Light of Eternity

PART III

PAYING THE PRICE

Living in the Light of Eternity

Chapter 8

LIVING FOR ANOTHER KINGDOM

In northeast India there is a group of tribal people numbering well over 100,000. Traditionally, they are animists, worshiping nature and their ancestors, making all kinds of sacrifices. As far as anyone knew, there had never been a church established among these people. They lived in total spiritual darkness—until a young man named Anil heard a gospel radio broadcast.

Anil was a member of this tribe. One day, while he was listening to his radio, he heard a name he had never heard before—Jesus Christ. The voice went on to say that Jesus was God who became a man and died for sinners to save them. Anil was very curious, and he wrote a letter to the address given at the end of the program.

"I heard on the radio about Jesus Christ being

God," he wrote. "Can you send me a book about your God?"

A few weeks later a New Testament arrived for Anil, and he started reading it every day. Anil wanted to know more about Jesus, and as he read he grew more and more astounded. "How is it that this took place in history, and we don't know anything about it?" he asked himself.

Since he was still young and had no real authority in the community, Anil went to speak to the elders. "I received this book some time ago," he told them. "This book tells about a God named Jesus Christ." He told them about what he had been reading and submitted the New Testament to them.

The elders were very interested. They decided that Anil would come every day and read this book to them. He began in Matthew with the genealogy of Jesus but became so confused that he skipped to Matthew 5 and started there.

Every day Anil would meet with the elders, and they would read a few pages out of the New Testament. Within a few months' time the elders were saying to one another, "Here is a God who asks us to live for Him—but in return, He says He will live through us, and everything we do, He says He will do through us. That is a whole new concept. This is a loving God who died for us. But now He is living, so He is dead no longer."

The Holy Spirit worked in their hearts, one by one, drawing them to Himself. And the people of this tribe began to pray to Jesus. They never heard of the "Four Steps to Salvation," but they were coming to the knowledge of the Lord Jesus. They had a relationship with Him. Within one year, about two hundred people had come to faith in Christ.

Meanwhile, the elders had learned about baptism

through Anil's reading. They wanted to understand what it was all about, so they sent Anil to find someone who could tell them more. Anil traveled thirty kilometers, asking around, before he found an old man who was a missionary in that area.

"We are some people who read your Bible, and we believe in and pray to Jesus. But now we have read about baptism. Could you tell us more about this and baptize us?" he asked.

But the man was physically unable to travel the distance to baptize these new believers, so Anil went home. When they heard this, the tribal elders decided to send fifty to sixty believers at a time to this old missionary so that he could baptize them! Approximately three hundred believers were baptized in this manner.

After a while the elders turned to Anil and told him, "When you were a young boy, we sent you out to learn to read and write, to become educated. You are the hope and the future of our tribe. Anil, you must now go someplace where you can learn more about this God, and then you can return and tell us."

Anil decided that he would leave his community, his wife and his child to learn more about Jesus. He had heard about a ministry in India that trained young people, so he wrote to them, requesting to be part of their training program.

Anil never mentioned that he was married and had a child. He never told them about the conversion of his tribe, because he felt no one would understand. He desperately wanted the training and didn't want anything to interfere with it. His plan was to learn as much about Jesus as he could, and then return and tell his people.

Soon a letter arrived, telling Anil that he was accepted for their year-long training program and could come right away.

During his year with the team, Anil soaked up as much as he possibly could. He kept his identity a secret until one night, during a prayer meeting, he began to pray and, without thinking, poured his heart out to the Lord for his people.

The leaders looked at each other and thought, This is a strange prayer. He's talking about the V__ tribe!

Afterward, they called Anil. "Brother, are you from the V__ tribe?" they asked him. He paused, swallowed and said, "Yes, I am."

That was all it took for Anil to open his heart to them, and they were astounded to hear of the great moving of God among his people.

Today there is a thriving, growing church among the V__ tribal people. Hundreds are coming to Christ and being baptized. Dozens of young people from the tribe are ready and willing to go into full-time ministry to serve the Lord. The entire community has been impacted with the Word of God.

Come, Follow Me

How rarely do we find people among us like Anil and the tribal believers who take the Word of God seriously! The Holy Spirit touches their hearts, and they wholly commit their lives to Him. They follow Jesus because He said, "Come, follow Me." Whatever He asks them to do, they will do it. It's as simple as that.

We see the same response from the disciples when Jesus called them.

"Now as he walked by the sea of Galilee, he saw Simon and Andrew his brother casting a net into the sea: for they were fishers. And Jesus said unto them, Come ye after me, and I will make you to become fishers of men.

"And straightway they forsook their nets, and followed him.

"And when he had gone a little farther thence, he saw James the son of Zebedee, and John his brother, who also were in the ship mending their nets.

"And straightway he called them: and they left their father Zebedee in the ship with the hired servants, and went after him" (Mark 1:16-20).

The word *straightway* simply means "immediately," "at once," or "directly." These men dropped everything they were doing and followed after Jesus.

I imagine that Zebedee, James and John's father, watched in consternation as his sons simply got up from their nets and followed Jesus. Perhaps he called after them. Perhaps he thought they had lost their senses.

The fact remains that Jesus said, "Come, and follow me. You could spend the rest of your life catching fish. But if you come after Me, I will make you fishers of men."

We Have His Example

That call is still real for those who claim to be His followers.

Peter states, "For even hereunto were ye called: because Christ also suffered for us, leaving us an example, that ye should follow his steps" (1 Pet. 2:21).

Jesus told His disciples, "A new commandment I give unto you, That ye love one another; as I have loved you, that ye also love one another" (John 13:34).

Jesus gave us the perfect example in His own life here on earth. If you were to read straight through the four Gospels, you would clearly see how He lived His life. It is summed up in this statement: "The Son of

Man came not to be ministered unto, but to minister, and to give his life a ransom for many" (Matt. 20:28).

"My purpose here," Jesus says in this passage, "is not for Myself. I did not come here so that everyone could gather around Me and treat Me well and take good care of Me. No—I came as the poorest of the poor. I came to suffer and die for others."

I remember a story I once heard about William Booth, the founder of the Salvation Army. At the time, he was an old, weak man. He was expected to speak at a huge convention, but because of his physical condition he was unable to go at the last minute. Instead, he sent a telegram.

Thousands gathered at the convention, eager to hear this great man of God speak. That night, at the appointed moment, someone came to the platform with the sealed telegram in his hand and explained that William Booth was unable to be there, but that he had sent a message to be read. As he opened the seal, the crowd grew hushed in expectancy.

There was only one word in the telegram: "Others."

That was all Booth wrote. What was he saying to them? "Remember, while you hold this great convention and enjoy the food, the good fellowship, and the laughter—remember, my message is still unchanged: others."

If we are followers of Jesus, it is this mind set that must govern all of our thinking. To be like Jesus is to be others-centered.

Learning from His Life—and Death

Jesus did not train His disciples in a classroom. He taught them through His example. He lived His life before them and willingly laid it down as well.

It is no wonder then that after they were filled with the Holy Spirit, the disciples remembered Jesus' words to go into all the world and preach the gospel. And they obeyed.

Every one of Jesus' disciples laid down his life for preaching the gospel. At first this seems a bit strange. After all, these men had walked and lived with Jesus for three years. They had seen miracles almost beyond belief. If any would, they would be the ones with great faith. We almost expect to read that they were supernaturally translated to heaven, not that they died criminals' deaths.

One of the disciples, Thomas, journeyed to India and preached the gospel there. One of the seven churches he planted is located less than five kilometers from where I was born and raised. Thomas laid down his life for Jesus in India.

At one time I thought that John was the only disciple who wasn't martyred, but I learned that he was also beheaded.

How could these men travel to places and do things that they knew would put their very lives at risk? Because Jesus was their example.

Jesus had never been the kind of Master who told them, "Don't do what I do, just do what I say." No— He said, "Come, and follow Me."

"Verily, verily," He told them, "I say unto you, He that believeth on me, *the works that I do shall he do also;* and greater works than these shall he do; because I go unto my Father" (John 14:12).

Turning the World Upside Down

I remember studying the book of Acts in Bible college. As we went through it, I thought it was a fascinating piece of history. But it is so much more than just history. The book of Acts is a living, open-ended book. Its story continues even today in the lives of committed believers. It is a book filled with people who were absolutely sold out, who had only one thing on their minds: Jesus died, He rose again, He is our Lord, He is coming back—let us tell our generation!

These people unselfishly abandoned their lives to communicate this message. When they were persecuted, beaten up, stoned, misunderstood and mistreated, they did not go around mourning their losses and licking their wounds. They went right back out and preached the gospel. I am not talking about just the apostles. These were the believers—everyday, "normal" people like you and me.

When we read about Jesus' life and are challenged to follow in His footsteps, we often feel overwhelmed. "Well, I can't help it," we rationalize, "I'm only a human being. Jesus is God—how can I expect to keep up with Him?" We so easily excuse ourselves from total commitment.

Then we come to Paul. It's not easy to write Paul off, because he was just as human as we are. "For I know that in me (that is, in my flesh,) dwelleth no good thing," he wrote in Romans 7:18. He considered himself an earthen vessel (see 2 Cor. 4:7).

Paul recognized that in his own strength he started from zero. He confessed his weaknesses and inadequacies continually. This is a man who argued with Barnabas, his coworker. Acts 15:39 tells us that "the contention was so sharp between them, that they departed asunder one from the other."

But for this normal human being named Paul, following Jesus was not a job that had a finishing point—nor was it a nine-to-five job. This was everyday life for him.

Let's look at an incident that took place in Paul's life when he came to Thessalonica.

"But the Jews which believed not, moved with envy, took unto them certain lewd fellows of the baser sort, and gathered a company, and set all the city on an uproar, and assaulted the house of Jason, and sought to bring them [Paul and Silas] out to the people.

"And when they found them not, they drew Jason and certain brethren unto the rulers of the city, crying, These that have turned the world upside down are come hither also" (Acts 17:5-6).

If you keep on reading, you will discover that this incident was one of many for Paul, and that it seemed an everyday occurrence in his Christian walk.

He was accused by the crowd of having turned the world upside down. But to Paul, this was simply part of following Jesus.

There was no dichotomy in Paul's life, or in the lives of the early believers. Their lives were not compartmentalized into "spiritual" and "secular" activities. Their whole existence was a solid commitment, a life totally given for the Lord and for His kingdom's sake.

Carefully Divided Lives

Unfortunately, most modern-day Christians seem satisfied with only *knowing* what these New Testament believers did and neglect to follow the example they provide.

The curse upon our lives as modern Christians is that we have very carefully divided the spiritual and the secular parts of our lives. On certain days we feel holy and wonderful. Our emotions are elevated, and we are ready to face any trials that may come—we're going to conquer the world for the Lord! On other days, back on the job and in the world, we say to ourselves, *How can I do all that for the Lord? I'm doing the best I can as it is.*

Somehow we have become very comfortable with living this divided life. But this is not what God has called us to be!

When we read about the uproar over Paul in Thessalonica, we have a difficult time relating to the treatment the believers received. We don't face this kind of persecution and opposition in our lives.

For the New Testament believers, *normal, everyday living for Jesus brought on persecution.* These people lived in a community and worked faithfully at their jobs every day. Nothing about them stood out, except the fact that they took the words of Jesus seriously, and they followed Him. This was the charge brought against them in Thessalonica.

The reason these believers lived was not to sew tents, to teach school or to construct buildings. These activities were simply their means of making a living.

But the kind of life they lived didn't stop when no one bought tents anymore, when they were too exhausted to lay another brick or when they retired. Their lives went on forever into eternity. While these believers lived on earth, their occupation was so temporal, so insignificant compared to what they saw as their primary responsibility. They lived for another kingdom.

As we read through the book of Acts, it's almost as if these believers were living in the midst of a whirlwind. Wherever they went they caused some kind of commotion or turmoil or trouble—simply because they lived what they believed.

We don't read passages like this in the book of Acts: "And they gathered together for committee meetings, ten people with long faces drinking black coffee with no sugar because they all were watching their diets.

"And one spoke up, saying, 'Brothers, God is saying to us that we should do such-and-such.'

"Yet another one responded, 'I am not sure. We should think about it some more. We are in so much debt right now—maybe we should vote on it.'"

So it goes in the lives of countless churches today! But you will not find committee meetings in the book of Acts. Instead, you will discover long hours of prayer. You will find fasting and waiting upon God to move.

And then, as you watch these believers move out into the marketplace, into their neighborhoods and their workplaces, you see them completely turn their communities upside down. Things changed when these men and women were around. These believers were world revolutionaries!

We have organized ourselves so much in the church today that often the Holy Spirit can no longer use us to change the world around us. We read the New Testament, and we are so intent on finding the hidden meanings behind the facts that we forget to look at the facts themselves! The believers of Acts were common people, just like us. But wherever they went, things invariably happened.

Looking at Jesus' life, we cannot ignore the fact that He too was a revolutionary. Wherever Jesus went, nothing was ever the same. He saw the darkness, the condition of the lost. And His life was driven by that which He saw.

This is how the Lord wants us to live our lives as well—as world revolutionaries who cannot help but change the world around us because of the lives we live.

We Know Too Much

The call of Christ still comes ringing in our ears today—"Come follow Me; and I will make you fishers of men." Jesus is not playing games with us. And hell is no joke—hell is real. I tell you, if you examine yourself and discover that you really do not believe what you claim to believe, you might as well get out of this whole business.

But if we truly believe what we say we believe, let us be different. We cannot live for ourselves anymore—we have been given too much knowledge for that. And for those to whom much is given, much will be required (see Luke 12:48). We must think carefully and plan deliberately to live our lives in such a way that they will make a difference.

Tens of thousands of missionaries must be sent to the harvest fields, and senders are needed to pray for and support them. Broadcasts need to be aired to the unreached nations; millions of Bibles need to be distributed.

What is missing? People who are willing to pray, to stand behind those who have gone to the mission field. People who are called and willing to go themselves.

If you want to be a world revolutionary—if you truly desire to live for another kingdom—then your service for the Lord can never be just a few hours of work every day. *It must be your life.*

Chapter 9

REVOLUTIONIZED FROM WITHIN

The small island nation of Sri Lanka, located off the southeastern tip of India, was in the throes of civil war for a decade. Tens of thousands of innocent people were butchered as two separate races fought for what they both believed was rightfully theirs.

These groups were involved in terrorist, guerilla-type warfare; they were ruthless in their attacks and totally committed to their cause.

Countless Sri Lankans fled the island and the violence, seeking refuge in India. Many native missionaries ministered to these refugees, who lost literally everything in order to escape with their lives.

On one of my visits to these refugees, one brother took me to a nearby camp. My eyes were opened to the horrible reality of what the war had done to these people. I saw ten-by-twelve-foot rooms with bare concrete walls, no windows and only a door for ventilation and light. There was no cooling or heating, no running water. I saw thirty or more people crammed into each of these rooms. I honestly do not know how a person could survive in those conditions.

As we went from room to room, the missionary pointed out certain people to me: "That man is a medical doctor. His wife and children were killed....See him? He is a lawyer. That one over there is a teacher...."

I looked around and saw men and women who had lived in the uppermost class of their society, now totally brought to ruin by the war. The doctor sat in a corner, wearing the only piece of clothing he owned; he was dirty, unshaven and depressed. I am sure he was dreaming of his wife and children, lamenting that they were no longer with him.

Who killed the people? Who drove them out? Terrorists.

These terrorists were so bent on achieving their goal that they would stop at nothing—they were ready even to die for their cause. I am told that many of them carried a cyanide pill, for use if they were captured by their enemies. I read in an Indian newspaper some time ago that thirty to forty of these terrorists died in a month's time. They were caught and arrested but committed suicide before anyone could gather any information.

I recently read about one group's recruiting practices. Four or five of them would drive a jeep into a remote but populated part of the country. They would set up loudspeakers in the public market, which blared out their message to the people. Finally, when a large crowd gathered, the group would offer this challenge:

"We challenge you parents to give up your sons, and you will remember forever a people who laid down their lives for the future of our nation. We challenge you young people to come forward and give your lives for this cause. We challenge you mothers to offer your children for our people."

I could scarcely believe what I read next: Young people stepped forward, and mothers with thirteen- and fourteen-year-old sons came up, pushing them and saying, "Go, go!"

The group would load up the recruits in the jeep and then drive off, never to be seen again.

"What kind of creatures are these people?" we say to ourselves.

I will tell you what they are. They are people totally committed to a kingdom here on earth—a kingdom that will eventually totter and perish.

If we as believers were to live by the things we know, committed to a heavenly kingdom, we would become radical revolutionaries. And our lives would affect not only our home, our community, our town, our state and our country—but the entire earth as well.

The Fires of Practical Living

The Bible is full of illustrations of two groups of people. There are those who know the truth and say, "Lord, Lord," but who demonstrate by their very lives that they don't really mean it.

Then there is a group of people who say, "Lord, Lord," and follow His footsteps. These are the people who have counted the cost. They look straight at the cross and gladly accept the pain, the inconveniences and the price they must pay to follow the Lord.

We read of the faith of these people in Hebrews 11. Their faith cost them everything! But they remained a group of people who changed the course of their generation.

C.S. Lewis once said, "Active habits are strengthened by repetition but passive ones are weakened. The more often [a man] feels without acting, the less he will be able ever to act, and in the long run, the less he will be able to feel."[1]

How true this is. God's Word says that we must be "doers of the word, and not hearers only" (James 1:22).

A.W. Tozer wrote this in his book *The Root of the Righteous*:

"We can prove our faith by our committal to it, and in no other way. Any faith that does not command the one who holds it is not a real belief; it is a pseudo belief only. And it might shock some of us profoundly if we were brought suddenly face to face with our beliefs and forced to test them in the fires of practical living.

"Many of us Christians have become extremely skillful in arranging our lives so as to admit the truth of Christianity without being embarrassed by its implications.

"So wide is the gulf that separates theory from practice in the church that an inquiring stranger who chances upon both would scarcely dream that there was any relation between them. An intelligent observer of our human scene who heard the Sunday morning sermon, and later watched the Sunday afternoon conduct of those who had heard it would conclude that he had been examining two distinct and contrary religions.

"Christians habitually weep and pray over beautiful truth, only to draw back from that same truth when it comes to the difficult job of putting it in practice." [2]

When you read the New Testament with a willing and an open heart, the gospel will penetrate your very life and break it open. It will touch your eyes, your ears, your hands and your legs. It will impact every part of you. You will become a vessel in the Lord's hands, pouring out your prayers, your finances, your reputation, your life-style—and ultimately your very life.

Do you see what happens when the gospel impacts your life? You become an all-out revolutionary.

Implementing the Revolution

My son Daniel has always been fascinated with how things work. One of his favorite things to do is to take something apart and tinker with it. He is always inventing, or reinventing, some little gadget.

One of his latest attempts was in making firecrackers. He would take matches and break off the heads; then he would roll them up in some paper and light it, hoping for an explosion.

To this day I have not seen one of those "firecrackers" actually explode like one. On the outside, each one looked like a firecracker, but it never actually was one. Why? What he rolled up inside lacked the substance of a true firecracker.

How do we take our knowledge of what the gospel can do and implement it practically? Knowledge brings responsibility; but finding a way to apply it practically is not always easy. It does no good to look right on the outside but lack the true power within. Just like Daniel's firecrackers, we will be duds.

Superstars Need Not Apply

In my own life, I have seen time and time again how God can use a nobody to make a difference.

Sometimes I feel so insecure. At other times I feel overwhelmed with all that I know needs to be done. And my wife knows sometimes I get upset with her and have to ask for forgiveness later.

What do I do when I struggle and fail? Where do I go?

To the cross! How many times? Many times a day, if needed. But the cross is the place where I can go and say, "Lord, I am Yours—along with all my weaknesses. But Your grace alone is what I need to serve You."

The Lord does not ask you to be a superstar. If you truly desire to be a revolutionary, all He desires is a weak, brokenhearted child who will surrender at the foot of the cross. All the Lord is looking for is a small group of people who will give their weaknesses to Him so that He can use them.

Let the Weak Say, "I Am Strong"

Look at Gideon's life in the book of Judges. The army of the Midianites had invaded Israel, and they were plundering everything in sight. We are told that "Israel was greatly impoverished because of the Midianites" (Judg. 6:6).

Gideon was threshing his wheat in a winepress, to hide it from the army, when an angel suddenly appeared to him. What did the angel say when he called Gideon? Did he say, "You scared rat, you good-for-nothing, you runaway"?

No. The angel told Gideon, "The LORD is with thee, thou mighty man of valour" (Judg. 6:12).

Gideon probably thought, "Who is he talking to? It could never be me. Doesn't he see that I'm hiding from the Midianites? He must know I'm scared to death."

But the Lord tells Gideon, in essence, "Yes,

Gideon—that's the way you see yourself. But I say, 'Let the weak say, I am strong.' How? It is 'not by might, nor by power, but by my spirit'" (Joel 3:10, Zech. 4:6).

No More Games

The other day I saw a painting that brought tears to my eyes. It is a nighttime scene, with a little boy asleep in his bed. He is clutching his little teddy bear as he sleeps peacefully and soundly. And there beside the bed is his father, kneeling and praying for him.

As I looked at that picture, I thought of the many times I have knelt beside my son's bed and prayed, "O God, let him live for You."

This is the life God is calling all of us to live. Become a revolutionary! Live your life with the same heartfelt urgency this father felt for his son.

Do you have a family member who doesn't know Jesus? Begin to pray for him or her. Commit yourself to fast for them. Pray for your children, your co-workers, your community—for the world.

Half of the the world has never heard the name of Jesus—thousands are plunging daily into hell! We must change the course of our generation. We can do it.

But how? A few more dollars? Yes, money would help. But, oh, that your heart would be changed—revolutionized! Before you even think about giving your money, your heart must already be broken for the lost.

Perhaps you feel you are useless to the Lord, that you are not good enough, or that you've already wasted your life.

Did you know that every day with Jesus is a new beginning? The Lord tells us that His mercies are new every morning. Whether you have lost seven days or seventy years, the Lord says to you, "Turn ye even to me with all your heart ... and I will restore to you the years that the locust hath eaten" (Joel 2:12,25).

The Lord never condemns you! He never says, "You didn't make it this time, so you lost out." No. Whether you succeed or fail, you are still in His hand.

Are you tired of fooling with the world? Are you tired of living just like everybody else? Do you desire the life of a revolutionary for the Lord?

Take the time to learn to pray. Commit your life daily for His kingdom's sake. Be a revolutionary. Be someone people will talk about when you walk by: "There goes someone who turns the world upside down!" Don't be satisfied with your own little society. Invest your life into a lost and dying world.

Come before the presence of the Lord and tell Him you are ready to stop playing games. No more pretend Christianity—you mean business. You are committing yourself to living for, not just knowing about, another kingdom—His kingdom.

You are no longer satisfied with knowing all the answers. Now you want to make some serious decisions for your life, starting today, by God's grace.

This is what God is looking for. He is not looking for a large number of strong, wealthy, confident people. He is looking for those who come to Him with their inadequacies and weaknesses, ready to be filled with His power and change the world. He is looking for you.

This is a new day for you to begin making changes in those areas of your life that have not been surrendered to the Lord. And I can assure you—His grace is sufficient.

Chapter 10

A LIVING SACRIFICE

The girl was barely fourteen years old when her parents sent her and her older sister to a Christian youth camp for two weeks. There she realized her need for Jesus and made a serious commitment to Him.

A few days later this young girl knew that the Lord was calling her to serve Him in missions. After that, her life radically changed. Everything she did was based on one question: Does this fall in line with my calling from the Lord?

When she went home, her parents knew something was different about her. Her life had been impacted dramatically. She devoured the Word of God each day. She spent much time in prayer. Jesus was real to her, and she learned to love Him more deeply as time went by.

This girl's parents had a dream that someday she would be able to attend the university and receive the best education available. The family as a whole enjoyed a respectable status in the community, and they cultivated a taste for many of the good things in society.

These parents planned for each of their daughters to enter a special finishing school, where they would take classes to learn the cultural graces that would accompany their debut into society. Hopefully, with these skills, both sisters would eventually marry well-to-do men from good families and make their parents proud.

However, the younger daughter felt that she could not be involved in some of the social activities like everyone else. When the time came for the sisters to enroll, she spoke to her parents. "I belong to Jesus," she told them, "and I have given my life to be a missionary someday. I cannot go to this school."

Of course, her parents were confused; and as she grew into a deeper relationship with Jesus, her life became even more of a puzzle to them.

This young girl had also made a decision before the Lord that she would never date in order to find a husband. Since the Lord knew every hair on her head, He would surely provide a husband for her. If this was the extent of God's care for her life, He knew that she would need a husband when she was old enough. She felt no need to go out and "shop around" to find a husband.

Finally her parents began to wonder if something was actually wrong with their younger daughter. They asked her, "Why are you acting so different? We can't understand you anymore. Look at your sister—she is acting perfectly normal." Her sister had a new boyfriend every week.

The girl continued to develop her walk with Jesus. She spent hours in her room, reading her Bible and praying—much of it for missions. By the time she was seventeen or eighteen, she had read over one hundred books on various cultural groups and missions.

One day she took a little coin from a foreign country and bored a hole into it. Then she took a leather string and tied that coin around her neck. "Now," she said, "every time I look into the mirror or feel this coin around my neck, it is a reminder to me that I am set apart by the Lord. Twenty-four hours a day, I am not my own. I must live to reach the lost."

The girl chose to go to nursing school, for she felt it would give her an advantage on the mission field. As her graduation day neared, her parents and friends approached her. "Now that you are finally through with your studies, you should at least take a small vacation and earn a little money before you leave, don't you think?"

However, she felt differently. "I have waited so long to be able to serve the Lord—how can I delay any longer?" The day she graduated, her bags were packed and she left to join a mission team.

A few years later, while this young woman was serving on the mission field, she met a young, skinny Indian named K.P. Yohannan. She knew that this was the man God had chosen for her to marry.

Gisela's willingness to set herself apart for Jesus, even at a young age, is what has given her the strength to withstand enormous tests and trials over the years.

What Will You Do with Yourself?

"I beseech you therefore, brethren, by the mercies of God, that ye present your bodies a living sacrifice, holy, acceptable unto God, which is your reasonable service. And be not conformed to this world: but be ye transformed by the renewing of your mind, that ye may prove what is that good, and acceptable, and perfect, will of God" (Rom. 12:1-2).

There have been many sermons, many explanations, and much exposition on these two verses from Romans. One thing is clear: Whether you were saved last night or fifty years ago, these verses are a call for total, absolute surrender of yourself to God.

You have been given one life, and the choice is yours as to how you will live it.

What will you do with yourself? That's a good question. E. Stanley Jones addresses some of the choices the world makes in his book *Victory Through Surrender*:

"Many ancient systems have come to the question of what is to be done with the self and have come to many differing answers. The answers coming out of the East have been, in large measure, answers that show world-weariness.

"Buddha focused this pervasive disillusionment about the self into the decisive sentence: 'Existence and suffering are one.' As long as you are in existence you are in suffering. Then the only way to get out of suffering is to get out of desire.... So cut the root of desire, become desireless even for life....

"Buddha would get rid of the problems of the self by getting rid of self.

"Vedantic [Hindu] philosophy says that Brahma is the only reality. But Brahma is the Impersonal. So the devotee sits and in meditation affirms: 'Aham Brahma'—I am Brahma. He tries to pass from the personal self to the Impersonal Essence, Brahma. When that transition is made ... the problems of the self are over.

"I asked [a devotee] his name and he replied:

'Ram, Ram.' I asked him where he had come from and he replied, 'Ram, Ram.' Where was he going? 'Ram, Ram.' What did he want? 'Ram, Ram.' I could get not other reply, for he had vowed to use no name except 'Ram, Ram.' This was high devotion, but very expensive to the self—it was gone. His face was expressionless. Rama was everything—he was nothing.

"When we turn from this world-weariness ... of the East to modern psychology we find a complete reversal of the attitudes toward the self. Modern psychology has three affirmations about the self: know thy self; accept thy self; express thy self.

"What is basically wrong with these three affirmations about the self? Take the first: know thy self. But how can you really know your self by studying your self in relation to your self, and other human selves, in a purely material environment? It is all earth-bound, lacks any eternal meaning or goal.

"Second: accept thy self. But how can you accept an unacceptable self, a self full of conflicts and contradictions, full of guilt and frustrations, inferiorities and inhibitions, full of its self? To ask a man to accept himself—that kind of self—is to ask the impossible.

"Third: secular psychology says: Express thy self. But if you have a dozen people together all of whom have been taught to express themselves—what have you got?...You have the stage set for clash and confusion and jealousy and strife."[1]

What will you do with yourself? Many say, "Who knows?" Today, man is still in darkness, trying to figure out the meaning and purpose of life.

Jesus told His disciples, "If any man will come after me, let him deny himself, and take up his cross daily, and follow me" (Luke 9:23). If you look closely at what Jesus is saying, you will discover that no matter what you try to do with yourself, whether you deny it, obliterate it, annihilate it, accept it or express it—believe me, it is still alive and kicking.

All That I Am for Christ

But Christ tells us what to do with ourselves: "Let Me live in you and through you." Paul expressed it beautifully in his letter to the Galatians: "I am crucified with Christ: nevertheless I live; yet not I, but Christ liveth in me" (2:20).

With life in Christ, my self is no longer the one that directs me and dictates to me. Now it is Christ, His will and His desire, living and acting through me. Jesus has asked us to love Him supremely, more than anything or anyone else.

But the questions still remain: How do we follow Christ? How do we live out this life?

This can only happen through an all-out surrender of ourselves to the Lord Jesus Christ. It means acknowledging the lordship of Christ in our lives, not just in theory but in practice. This is why the habit of compartmentalizing our lives must end. All of me, all that I am, belongs to Christ.

It is a daily practice to learn this principle and live it out in our lives. The choice we make is not a collective one. It is not one we make as a church, a family or even a couple. It is an individual choice.

Self-help Spirituality

The problem with you and me, and with the culture in which we are immersed, is that we are taught basically to do everything for ourselves—including becoming more spiritual. Whether it means training your children, loving your spouse, living a single Christian life, overcoming weight problems or dealing with past griefs, we are taught that we can do it all by ourselves.

If you don't believe me, take a closer look at your local Christian bookstore on your next visit. You will find that many high-selling books these days center around self-help and recovery programs.

If we take this approach to spiritual living, we will suddenly find ourselves out of focus. We will no longer take the Bible at face value. Instead, we will be using it to find scriptures that justify our need for happiness and make our life more comfortable here on planet Earth.

Suddenly we discover that we are no longer centering around Jesus and His will for our lives, but we are using Him as a means of comfort in the here and now. We take what the world offers us and we put a label on it to "Christianize" it, whether it be heavy-metal music, aerobic videos or color coordination seminars.

Our children also assimilate the culture into their life-styles. As we watch them head toward the ways of this world, all we do is shrug our shoulders helplessly and say, "Well, what can we do? It's our culture."

What is happening here? We look around for ways to uphold our life-style and our culture. We have allowed ourselves to be deceived by the society in which we live, and by other's opinions and teachings. We look for Bible verses that carry even the faintest resemblance to approval of our life-styles.

During one of my recent meetings in a church, one man made a comment that gave me some insight on the workings of our human nature:

"I am a medical doctor," he told me. "If I were to live the life-style that you preach about, I wouldn't be able to keep my practice. I own a home and a car. If I were to reduce my standard of living as you suggest, my colleagues wouldn't take me seriously anymore. I don't even think they'd want to come into my house.

"I have to live this kind of life-style if I am to be accepted in the medical community."

Do you see how he was defending and justifying himself in order to maintain his life-style? However, I knew that arguing with him was not the answer.

"You make your decision," I responded. "All I can give you are some basic principles. You have to work it out in your own life."

Lord, What Do You Want Me to Do?

I once heard Billy Graham say that the hardest thing for a man to do is to give away his money. When I first heard that, I thought to myself, That statement makes no sense. How can that be?

But then he went on to say that a man's money represents his ambitions, his dreams, his toil, his priorities, his time, his activities, his motives— everything. And for someone to take his money and give it away without expecting a reward here and now is not an easy thing to do.

It is extremely easy to justify our own needs and comforts. But when it comes to sacrificing and giving to extend the Lord's kingdom, all of a sudden we must pray about it. When it has to do with our own comforts and pleasures, we seldom seek the counsel of the Lord.

When Paul gave his life to the Lord, the first question out of his mouth was, "Lord, what wilt thou have me to do?" (Acts 9:6). This is the question we must also ask.

What went through your mind when you read Gisela's story at the beginning of this chapter? Perhaps it sounded radical to you. Perhaps you had a hard time relating to her situation at all.

When you say that you have given your life to the Lord, understand this: It is not a one-time commitment. It is a daily choice, a daily taking up of the cross. Each and every day we must say to Jesus, "Lord, today I am Yours. My soul, my body, my spirit; my wealth, my children, my husband, my wife—all that I have, all that I am, is Yours today. What do You want me to do today? How do You want me to live?" Allow the Holy Spirit to take the Word of God and weave it into the very fiber of your being. Allow Him to give you His guidance as you step out.

Perhaps you have had your eye on a new pair of shoes, or a suit coat or maybe even a new recliner for your living room. Is it too much for you to say, "Lord, this money is Yours, and my time is Yours. What do You want me to do?"

Then be still. Let the Lord speak to you.

You may well ask, "How will I hear His answer? How can I know it is the Lord?"

Many years ago I used to go to a barber who would cut my hair for twelve dollars, including the tip. At that time that was a good sum of money to spend on a haircut—but he always did a nice job.

I did know of another place that would do it for three bucks, but I always had the feeling that they would butcher my hair if I went in there!

At that time the Lord was teaching me this very principle: "If one hair on your head that falls off is so important to Me, you should know that I am concerned about everything in your life. Is it too much for you to ask Me what you should do with even one dollar or one hour?"

I began to understand that bringing my life before the Lord was not an unbearable burden and a chore; it was a wonderful privilege to listen to Him.

I took some time and prayed to the Lord about my haircut. "Lord," I prayed, "I have always made this decision with my rational mind. What do You want me to do?" I considered my options—basically it boiled down to twelve dollars or three. He was giving me a choice to make in the light of eternity. And I decided to go to the butcher!

It was much more simple than I expected. No one was hollering in my ear, "Go to this one!" I didn't have to hear an audible voice.

Because of the Holy Spirit He has given us, God clearly speaks to us as He did in the days of the New Testament. But He does not go around beating people on the head, saying, "Listen to Me!" He gives us a choice. All we have to do is ask Him, "Lord, what do You want me to do?"

Where Is the Practical Application?

Sincere believers will sometimes go forward in church, surrender their lives and make a full-time commitment to the Lord. But when they walk away, nothing is changed. Why? *There is no practical application.*

When your children ask you for money to buy something, why not say, "Let's pray about this and see what the Lord wants us to do with this money. You want these tennis shoes, but let's listen to what God tells us to do."

One day as I was talking to a dear brother who loves the Lord deeply, I saw his son walking by. I couldn't help but be shocked at his appearance. His hair had been cut so that one half of it was shaved off and the other half hung down in tails around his head.

I swallowed and commented to my friend, "Your son looks very interesting these days!"

"Well, you know, his friend got this haircut, and so he had to have it too," he explained.

I turned to my friend and asked, "Have you ever taken some time to be with your son and ask him, 'Son, why don't we pray about this haircut? Let's ask the Lord if He would have you get your hair cut in this manner.'"

My friend looked surprised. The thought had never occurred to him that a haircut was something he could pray about, much less with his son.

Please don't misunderstand me—I am not saying you should or shouldn't cut your hair in a certain manner. All I am asking is that we begin to think in these terms: "My life, and all that I am, belong to the Lord." We need to take what we know to be true and apply it in every area of our lives. The Lord is concerned about every decision we make.

Everything I write means nothing after you close this book, unless you begin to do something practical about it. We must daily ask the Lord, "What do You want me to do?"

Take a Closer Look

A young missionary lay on her deathbed in India. A friend came up to her and said, "You must feel a little sad to go so early."

She smiled and told him, "No. Death is mild. My job is finished. I am going to be with Jesus."

You see, once your life is given over completely to the Lord, you are no longer intimidated by circumstances or swayed by what others think. Paul said, "All things are yours, whether Paul, or Apollos, or Cephas, or the world, or life, or death, or things present, or things to come; all are yours; and ye are Christ's; and Christ is God's" (1 Cor. 3:21-23).

Paul also said, "All the promises of God in him [Jesus] are yea, and in him Amen" (2 Cor. 1:20).

When you understand who Christ is and you surrender your life to Him, you will recognize that He is no tyrant who sits on a high and mighty throne, shaking His finger at you and saying, "No!" Paul tells us that in Jesus all the promises of God are "Yes!"

When the Lord calls us to commit our life to Him as a living sacrifice, He desires a living, breathing, moving sacrifice. He desires a total surrender of the will, the intellect, the mind, our five senses, emotions and actions.

I pray that you will take a closer look at who you are. From now on you can live your life for a different purpose than just this world alone. I pray that you would begin to consider eternity as your perspective.

But I must also warn you: If this is your decision, know that you have chosen to walk a narrow road. When Jesus called His disciples to follow Him, there were some conditions He set before them. The choice we make to follow Christ involves a cost. There will be inconveniences, difficulties and pain. And Satan will counterattack your decision.

But, praise the Lord, whether you are standing or have fallen, you can rejoice because you have surrendered yourself to Him. When everything has been said and done, and the earth as we know it is only a memory, Jesus will say to you, "Well done, good and faithful servant." That is all that matters—His approval.

Chapter 11

SELLING ALL FOR THE PEARL

On August 27, 1990, at 6:10 a.m., my mother died. She was eighty-four. Her last words were, "I am going to my Father's house." She loved the Lord deeply and walked with Him very closely. Through her example she taught her six sons to love Jesus. Her twenty-one grandchildren and five great-grandchildren were touched by her love for the Lord as well.

I was on my way from India to South Korea to speak at a missions conference when she was admitted into the hospital with heart problems. I canceled my trip and stayed in India, visiting her daily, reading Bible verses and praying with her. As soon as I started reading a verse, she would usually finish the rest of it from memory.

For as long as I can recall, my mother would get up as early as four in the morning to read her Bible and pray. For hours she would pour her heart out to her loving Father and find strength and encouragement in His Word. Then she'd wake up the rest of the family and say, "Time to pray!" Every morning we'd sit in a circle together, read our Bibles and pray. I cannot remember a time in my life when I didn't see my mother with a Bible in her hands during the morning hours.

I remember so well the day my mother took me with her to a gospel meeting. I was only eight years old, but that day I gave my heart to Jesus.

Committing my life to serve the Lord at age sixteen was a direct answer to my mother's prayers. For three and a half years she had fasted and prayed every Friday, asking the Lord to call one of her boys to become a missionary.

Hardly a day went by that my mother didn't visit several homes in my village to witness about the Lord. Even as she lay in her hospital bed she talked continually about Jesus. The doctors, nurses and aides were all touched by her simple yet strong faith.

After her death, her doctors told me they had never seen such peace or assurance in a dying person as they had seen in her. "I am going home soon," she would tell them. "I am so happy."

The day before she died, one of the young doctors came to her bedside. She took his hand and told him, "You sit here and sing for me 'When the Roll Is Called up Yonder I'll Be There.'"

The next morning the phone rang. It was my older brother. "Our mother has just passed away," he said. She longed for her Father's house and had finally gone home.

Then came the funeral. Thousands of people

whose lives she had touched attended. It was the saddest day of my life.

Being the youngest son, it was my responsibility to go to the coffin just before it was closed and cover my mother's face with a veil. My oldest brother sat at the foot of the coffin.

As I lifted the veil, something struck me like lightning. When I looked at her face, I realized that something was missing.

Her earring was gone. I had never seen my mother without her earring. And the tiny gold chain that was the symbol of her marriage with my father—that was also missing from around her neck. And the ring on her finger that she always wore—it was gone too.

I hadn't thought about these things before. There had been too much going on. But now, in the last few seconds that I would see her on this earth, I noticed. And then, as I placed the veil over her face, one other thing stood out to me—her Bible was not there.

Now the veil had been placed over her face, and the coffin was closed. The crowd quietly dispersed and our family slowly walked home.

It is a custom in my native place that when the father dies, the oldest son becomes the caretaker of the family. Ever since my father died in 1974, I have looked to my oldest brother as the head of our family. I ask his opinion in matters that pertain to our family, and I respect his wishes. My oldest brother was also the one who handled my mother's affairs after her death.

When we arrived home that afternoon, my brother took me aside. "I know you have to go overseas soon," he said. "But I thought you might like to know how much money our mother left in the bank."

I was curious. I imagined there would be a good sum of money, because we six children had given her quite a bit over the years.

149

"Well," he told me, "I looked through all her records, and she has about two or three dollars left."

"What?" I was astounded.

"Yes," he replied, "and she also kept a record of what she did with her money."

We never before knew what she did with it. I discovered that afternoon that over the years she had been faithfully sending her money to dozens of missionaries, Bible school students and others who were serving the Lord.

"Oh, and by the way," my brother added, "she wanted her earring, her gold chain and her ring to be sold, and the money used for mission work among the unreached."

I was quiet after I heard this information. This was not just another great illustration of a saint of God—this was my mother. It hit close to home, and I thought a lot about my own life afterward.

In the previous chapter I described how we give our lives to God as living sacrifices. Now I want to provide an eternal perspective on our material goods—and our families as well.

We cling to so many things in this world. But we will not carry them with us.

He Is the Owner

I know a close friend whose home was broken into several times in the past few years. Most of the time, he told me, they didn't find anything worth stealing! The damage they did to enter his home cost more money than the theft itself.

He told me, "Brother K.P., my main concern was not for the house but for my family. I was just glad they weren't at home when it happened.

"After the last attempt, I thought to myself, *Why*

not put a note on the door saying, 'Please come in—the door is unlocked. Take all you want.' There was really nothing to take!" he laughed.

"I found my imagination painting a picture of our house being dismantled by thieves, or burning to the ground. And I was pleased and surprised by my reaction to the whole mental scenario. Well, so what, I thought to myself. I am not the owner—the Lord owns this house. Whether it's torn apart or burnt to the ground—no problem. Where will we sleep tomorrow night? That's His problem."

Now What Do You Think?

One day as I sat in an airport terminal, waiting for a connecting flight, I agonized and prayed to the Lord over the many opportunities on the mission field. I thought particularly of the millions of Muslims throughout the world and the immense challenge before us to reach them with the gospel.

Suddenly it was as if I was taken away in my mind's eye to another time and place. A voice said, "Your son will finish high school and go to the mission field." As I looked, there was Daniel in Iran, going door to door and passing out gospel tracts. Then I saw him being arrested. They pushed him, blindfolded, up against a wall. Shots rang out, and he slumped over, blood pouring out of a fatal wound to his head.

I saw myself at home, hearing the news for the first time—in shock. Then the voice asked me, "Now what do you think?"

Back in the airport terminal again, the question wouldn't go away. What did I think? What would I do with my son?

From the very beginning Gisela and I have always told our children, "When you finish your studies, you can go to the mission field." Our children have always thought of their lives in terms of reaching the lost.

As I sat in the airport, I knew what my response would be. If Daniel went to Iran and distributed tracts door to door and then was caught and killed, all I could say would be, "Praise the Lord. He did what the Lord called him to do. He is not mine. My son belongs to the Lord."

Do I write these stories and scenarios just to impress you, or to fill up pages in a book? No.

What I want you to understand from all of these illustrations is this: Your choice to live for Jesus is not just an excuse to escape from hell. It is not just to have your sins forgiven, to have a nice, comfortable life here on earth with good fellowship and a free ride to heaven.

Life for Jesus is really a battleground. We are in the enemy's territory, and we are in an all-out war. If you want to know how to live practically for Jesus, read His life in the Gospels and follow His example. Day and night He was continually harassed by the powers of darkness and the enemies of the gospel.

Jesus never had a nice place to lay His head. He was misunderstood and rejected. He was left alone often. He died daily. Paul and the other apostles followed in those same footsteps.

Please don't misunderstand me—I am not saying you will be more spiritual if you walk around in rags and alienate yourself from society. But when you commit yourself to live for Jesus, you cannot be just like everyone else.

How to Purchase a Pearl

Jesus told a parable about a merchant looking for fine pearls. When he found a pearl of real worth, he sold everything he owned in order to buy the pearl. This is what the kingdom of God is like. Juan Carlos Ortiz, in his book *Call to Discipleship,* expands the story and gives us a better understanding of what total, absolute surrender is all about.

"So when man finds Jesus, it costs him everything. Jesus has happiness, joy, peace, healing, security, eternity. Man marvels at such a pearl and says, 'I want this pearl. How much does it cost?'

"The seller says, 'It's too dear, too costly.'

"'But how much?'

"'Well, it's very expensive.'

"'Do you think I could buy it?'

"'Oh, of course. Anybody can.'

"'But you say it's too expensive. How much is it?'

"'It costs everything you have—no more, no less—so anybody can buy it.'

"'I'll buy it.'

"'What do you have? Let's write it down.'

"'I have $10,000 in the bank.'

"'Good, $10,000. What else?'

"'I have nothing more. That's all I have.'

"'Have you nothing more?'

"'Well, I have some dollars here in my pocket.'

"'How many?'

"'I'll see: thirty, fourty, fifty, eighty, one hundred, one hundred twenty—one hundred twenty dollars.'

"'That's fine. What else do you have?'

"'I have nothing else. That's all.'

"'Where do you live?'

"'I live in my house.'

"'The house too.'

"'Then you mean I must live in the garage?'

"'Have you a garage, too? That too. What else?'

"'Do you mean that I must live in my car, then?'

"'Have you a car?'

"'I have two.'

"'Both become mine. Both cars. What else?'

"'Well, you have the house, the garage, the cars, the money, everything.'

"'What else?'

"'I have nothing else.'

"'Are you alone in the world?'

"'No, I have a wife, two children…'

"'Your wife and children too.'

"'Too?'

"'Yes, everything you have. What else?'

"'I have nothing else, I am left alone now.'

"'Oh, you too. Everything. Everything becomes mine: wife, children, house, garage, cars, money, clothing, everything. And you too. Now you can use all those things here, but don't forget they are mine, as you are. When I need any of the things you are using you must give them to me because now I am the owner.'"[1]

Be Led by the Holy Spirit

Every truth in this world can become a heresy or false doctrine if it is thrown off balance. If you look at the doctrine of any cult, you will find at least a grain of truth. But any truth stretched beyond its limits will become a false doctrine.

It isn't my desire that you take what I am writing and think that this is all there is to life in Christ. We must continue to follow the Lord closely, and He provides that daily balance we need.

This is why we are told in the Word of God, "For as many as are led by the Spirit of God, they are the sons of God" (Rom. 8:14).

As we walk through this life, we can be led by the Spirit, or we can be led by our own self, our logic, other people's opinions or our own flesh.

What led Mahatma Gandhi to live the way he lived, giving up everything to free India from colonial bondage? What led Buddha to give up his princely authority, his palace, his wife and child, to walk away from it all and live as a monk the rest of his life?

It was *not* the Holy Spirit. Their own selves—their own flesh—prompted their actions.

Our flesh will do a lot of good-looking things. The flesh can do a lot of praying. It can do a lot of fasting. It can give up everything. But what does the Word of God say about this? "And though I bestow all my goods to feed the poor, and though I give my body to be burned, and have not charity [love], it profiteth me nothing" (1 Cor. 13:3).

If we are not controlled and led by love, all of our outward behavior means absolutely nothing. Love, you see, is a fruit of the Holy Spirit. We must continually be filled with the Holy Spirit and daily led by Him.

What Will You Leave Behind?

"For what is your life?" asks James. "It is even a vapour, that appeareth for a little time, and then vanisheth away" (James 4:14).

Our life is so short. What will you leave behind?

My mother could not take her earring, her necklace, her ring—not even her Bible—with her when she died. But the faith she instilled in her children's and grandchildren's lives, and the lives of others she touched, will live forever.

What will you leave behind? A few pieces of jewelry, a house, some cars, some land or some money in a bank?

Or will you leave more than that?

What about a son or a daughter who is serving the Lord somewhere in the world? What about the memory that you lived for Jesus with all your heart—that you gave Him all you had and all you were to gain His kingdom? What about the knowledge that you gave all you could to win the lost and dying souls of the world?

May you find that willingness in your heart to sell all you have for that pearl of great price, to love Jesus more than anything else. Life is too short to make any other decision worthwhile.

Jesus told us that anyone who would follow Him must deny himself and take up his cross (see Matt. 16:24). In the next chapter I want to show you where Jesus focused. His eyes weren't on the cross—He looked beyond it.

Chapter 12

LOOK BEYOND THE CROSS

Before Samuel was called of the Lord to missionary work, he lived a very comfortable life in South India, making a good sum of money at his job. It was not a life anyone would want to leave—unless he were constrained by the love of the Lord.

Samuel was a believer and faithfully attended church. He read his Bible and prayed on a regular basis. When Samuel attended a Gospel for Asia missions conference in 1984, however, he was challenged to give his life to serve the Lord full-time.

There was no question that this was what Jesus wanted him to do. He went home, resigned his job and bought train tickets for himself and his family to the state of Karnataka.

Samuel chose one particular region in Karnataka because he had heard that this area was extremely unreached. It was also notorious for being one of the most vicious anti-gospel regions in the nation.

He managed to find a tiny hut they could call home, and gradually he learned the local language. As his language skills grew, he began to preach and witness in the community. One by one people came to know Jesus. A local church was established, and Samuel was able to construct a small building where he and the believers met for worship. Then came a day when Samuel led a Hindu priest to the Lord Jesus Christ.

Now, it is quite a daring thing to win your local Hindu priest to the Lord in a community where the vast majority are Hindus. It is particularly risky when your area is a stronghold for fanatical, militant Hinduism.

The news spread fast: "The local temple priest is no longer the temple priest—he is studying the Bible and sharing the gospel." The priest's own brothers contacted this militant group, specially trained in torture of those who violate their religion or disobey orders. The group's goal is to see India eventually become a completely Hindu nation. The gang reacted swiftly to the news.

One Sunday not long after, Samuel gathered the believers together as usual for worship and teaching. Suddenly a jeep pulled up in front of the building and stopped. A group of angry men got out and walked into the church, right up to Samuel. They beat him viciously with iron rods, smashing his hand and breaking his arm. His leg and his collar bone were also broken. Samuel's family and the other believers stood by helplessly, weeping at his terrible pain and the fact that they were unable to help him.

Suddenly Samuel's seven-year-old son ran up to the front. "Please don't kill our daddy!" he cried. The gang leader turned on this little boy and swung his iron rod. The boy screamed in pain as the rod connected with his back and broke it. He fell to the dirt floor like a crumpled rag.

The gang stepped back from their victims and snarled, "This is only a warning to you to stop preaching this Jesus. Next time we come back, we won't leave you alive. We will kill you and bury you in this place." They jumped in their jeep and drove off in a cloud of dust.

Samuel and his son were taken to a local hospital where they remained for several months.

A few months after this incident occurred, I was in India teaching at our local training center. Little did I know that Samuel had also arrived there to meet with our leaders.

That evening during the prayer meeting, the Lord strongly impressed upon my heart that I was to pray for anyone who needed healing. I stood up and said, "If anyone is sick tonight, no matter what it is, I want you to stand up. The Lord has promised us by His Word that He will heal—and He will heal you tonight."

Several in the group stood up, and one of them was Samuel, although I didn't know it at the time. As I prayed for each one, I knew the Lord would heal them.

The next day I found out that Samuel had arrived. I asked him to share his testimony during the evening meeting. I knew it would be a challenge and an encouragement to the young students at our training center who were planning themselves to go to the pioneer areas and witness for the Lord.

That evening, though, when he stood up, he added something to his testimony which I hadn't expected.

"Last night, before I came to your prayer meeting, I could not do anything with my hand," he said, showing us the one the Hindu gang had smashed. "I couldn't lift anything, I couldn't ride a bicycle and I couldn't even wring out a washcloth.

"When Brother K.P. prayed, the Lord healed me. Now I can carry a bucket, I can move my hand any way I want and I can wring out my washcloth. The Lord has healed me!" His testimony greatly moved the hearts of the students.

I spent some time with Samuel during those days, and I asked him, "What are you going to do now?"

This young missionary looked at me with a peaceful determination on his face and said, "I am going back. Even if I am killed, my blood will be the foundation for many more churches."

A few days later Samuel did go back. His little son is doing well and attends the local school. Since this incident took place, Samuel continues to share the gospel in that same area. He has baptized many more converts and has been beaten again.

This precious brother has counted the cost, and I know he is willing to pay the price.

I Would Find Some Excuse

Now tell me this: What would *you* do if you were in Samuel's place? If Hindu fanatics promised to come back and finish you off if you kept preaching the gospel, what would your response be?

I can tell you what I might want to do. I would look for a Bible verse that would justify my getting out—something like, "Then took they up stones to cast at him: but Jesus hid himself, and went out of the temple, going through the midst of them, and so passed by" (John 8:59).

Or I could find the one that says, "But if any provide not for his own, and specially for those of his own house, he hath denied the faith, and is worse than an infidel" (1 Tim. 5:8).

An infidel! Oh, my goodness—I'd better leave this place and take better care of my family. The Bible says so. Jesus left too, you know.

There must be hundreds of verses in the Bible I could isolate to justify my rational, sober-minded decision.

And, of course, my best argument would be something like this: "I'm only forty-some years old! God wants me to use my brain for His kingdom. With all the investment He has made in my life since I was sixteen, would it be right for me to be killed by some fanatics next week? Don't be stupid! I am going to leave this place so I will have another forty years of my life to invest in and build God's kingdom."

But what did Samuel say? "Even if I am killed, my blood will lay the foundation for many more churches." And he went back. No arguments, no excuses, no rationalizations.

In Acts 20, when Paul was headed to Jerusalem, the Holy Spirit revealed to him that he would be bound there and suffer greatly. Imagine with me the scenario that took place during this time.

Paul and the believers were in the middle of a prayer meeting when the Holy Spirit spoke through one of the believers: "This man Paul who is among you tonight will be bound and chained in Jerusalem. He will face afflictions and sufferings."

There was a shocked silence that followed the prophecy. For these believers, Paul was bigger than life. They were willing to die for him.

After the prayer meeting ended, a group gathered around Paul.

One elder said, "Paul, you know that the Holy Spirit spoke to you tonight."

"Yes," Paul replied, "I believe it was the Holy Spirit."

There was a collective sigh of relief among the group. "So," the man responded, "you will not be going to Jerusalem after all."

Another commented, "Now that the Lord has warned you, you can stay away from that city."

"I didn't say that," Paul told them. "I only said that I believe it is a word from the Lord. As a matter of fact, everywhere I have gone the Holy Spirit has said the same thing to me. I am going to Jerusalem—I must."

The voices of the believers rose together in protest: "Paul, you can't go...please! You are facing a threat to your life! Don't leave us, Paul."

Paul told them, "But, you see, I don't consider my own life dear to me. How can you kill a man who is already dead? I love my Lord more than life itself, and there are many who still need to know Him."

I am of the firm conviction that God wants to do something wonderful in our generation, with believers who are serious about following Him. He wants to reach every language, every tribe and every nation with the gospel. Right now I believe He is building the foundation to do that job through us, His children.

God is still looking for those who will share His heart. "And I sought for a man among them, that should make up the hedge, and stand in the gap before me for the land, that I should not destroy it: but I found none" (Ezek. 22:30).

Looking to Jesus

Recent studies of U.S. highways have shown an

astonishingly high incidence of roadside collisions—where drivers have collided with cars parked legally on the side of the road. Most of the drivers were not under the influence of alcohol or medication, and most of the collisions occurred during favorable weather conditions.

As safety experts studied these statistics and determined to account for the number of these collisions, they came up with a fascinating explanation: the moth effect.

Just as a moth is drawn unconsciously to a flame, a driver tends to steer his car involuntarily where his eyes are focused. Thus, if his vision locks onto a vehicle parked by the side of the road rather than focusing on the road in front of him, he will inevitably collide with the car.

We have to deal with a "moth effect" in our walk with the Lord as well. If we look back, or to the right or the left, we will not only stop moving forward, but we will begin to head in that direction. If we choose to obey and move out in faith, looking at Jesus, we will not only draw closer to Him, but we will also become more like Him.

"Let us run with patience the race that is set before us, *looking unto Jesus* the author and finisher of our faith; who for the joy that was set before him endured the cross, despising the shame, and is set down at the right hand of the throne of God. For consider him that endured such contradiction of sinners against himself, lest ye be wearied and faint in your minds" (Heb. 12:1-3).

This is the key—looking to Jesus. The Lord may ask us to do something that goes contrary to every grain of logic within us. Our emotions may be rising up in protest against it. Those around us may be doing their best to convince us to look back. The only way we will have the strength to do what God has asked us to do is by keeping our focus on Jesus!

As the author of Hebrews says, it is as if we are in a race. We have laid aside every encumbrance, and "the sin which doth so easily beset us." We have come to the point where we are willing to break away from the past and begin a new life in Jesus. As we run our race, we face hardships and distractions. Our enemy knows our weaknesses, and he tries his best to put us out of the race.

But as we strain our eyes, looking down the track to the finish line, we see someone familiar: it is Jesus! He has finished His race, and He is waiting for us there. Suddenly we realize that if He has already completed the race, so can we! As we focus our eyes on Him, all the other sounds and sights that distract us from our task fade away. We forget about our weariness as we run steadily toward the finish line, our eyes fixed on Jesus only.

Our race isn't yet completed. It is a daily, hourly, minute-by-minute choice we must make to keep looking forward. We can be sure there will be difficulties and distractions. We will stumble and fall sometimes, and we will have to repent for our sins. But we can be sure that Jesus will always be there, waiting for us at the finish line.

Paul told the Philippians that he knew he hadn't arrived spiritually; but "this one thing I do, forgetting those things which are behind, and reaching forth unto those things which are before, I press toward the mark for the prize of the high calling of God in Christ Jesus" (Phil. 3:13-14).

This is the secret to accepting the cross, to paying the price no matter how great it is or what others say. Jesus endured the cross, the pain, the agony, the shame and the suffering "for the joy that was set before him."

Jesus looked beyond the cross, and He saw the joy that was waiting. This is what enabled Him to endure the horrible suffering and death He experienced for us.

What will it take for us to be able to pick up our cross daily and follow Jesus? How can we possibly be able to pay the price that is required of us? We can only do it as we look beyond the cross and see the joy that is set before us. Joy that is indescribable, glorious. Joy that will make every ounce of suffering and inconvenience worth it all.

I do not know where you are in your spiritual life, or where you are coming from. But I pray that the enemy will not steal away your affection from the One who has paid with His blood to redeem you. I pray that you will not walk away from Him. I pray that you will be willing to pay the price in order to follow Jesus.

Every day eighty thousand souls slip into hell for all eternity. They have never heard the gospel.

It is for them we must live. It is for them we must breathe. It is for them we must give up the comfortable life this world offers us. For them we must be willing to live lives that people misunderstand. We must be willing to walk away from all that we could accumulate on this earth and be content with what the Lord gives us.

While you are on this earth, make this your life's ambition: to bring as many souls as possible with you.

God will give you the grace to live this life as He calls you. In the light of eternity, the battle is really not that long. I pray that you will look beyond the cross, beyond the pain and sacrifice, and see Jesus, who is waiting there for you. The joy which awaits you will be far greater than any price you have to pay.

Living in the Light of Eternity

PART IV

THE SECRET OF VICTORY

Chapter 13

STANDING ON EMPTINESS

I stood up in my hotel room and put the phone down on the receiver—hard. I had just talked with our headquarters in India, and what I had just heard was outrageous. I wanted to do something about it, but there was nothing I could do until I was in India on my next trip. I sat down on the bed and stewed over the information.

Moses Paulose, one of our most respected native missionary leaders, has a ministry on the Hindu pilgrimage island of Rameswaram, off the southeastern tip of India. Each year millions of devout Hindus flock to the island in hopes that their sins will be forgiven when they bathe in what they consider to be the sacred waters of the Indian Ocean. Paulose and his team are able to reach out to people from nearly every language group in the Indian subcontinent as a result.

A few months prior to this telephone call, we had arranged for Paulose to take a group of young people from several Bible schools for a summer of practical training. I knew that if anyone could teach these students the meaning of discipleship, it would be Paulose.

This phone call had informed me that by the end of the first month, over 70 percent of these young people had left! One day when Paulose arrived home, he discovered that the last of the deserters had sneaked out, bought a train ticket with some borrowed money and taken off.

Only one or two ended up staying for the entire summer. One young man from my village had been with Paulose. When I saw him, I was shocked. Normally I would consider him skinny anyway, but after his time in Rameswaram he looked as if he had lost half his weight!

When I discovered all this information, I was very angry. After all, we had invested time, energy and our reputation to send these Bible school students for training. We had sent money to Paulose for their food and other necessities. Why on earth was he treating them so badly? Why did he let them get out of the battle? There were some tremendous opportunities that now looked completely lost to me.

The more I thought about it, the angrier I became. I resolved to confront Paulose the next time I saw him.

Sure enough, the next time I traveled to India I met Paulose the very first week. Without even asking him how his ministry was going, I jumped on him. I vented all my frustrations about this failed ministry opportunity and his manner of training these students. On and on I went.

Moses Paulose has a perpetual smile on his face. If you have something to say, he will listen until you are through. Then, very calmly and quietly, he will speak just a few sentences. And when he is finished, you do not know what else to say.

I finished my tirade, accusing him quite justly, I felt, of what seemed to be poor judgment on his part.

In his quiet way, Paulose simply said, "Do you know that when I expect seventy people to come with me for training, I realize even before they arrive that only a handful will make it?"

Incredulous I said, "Paulose, what are you talking about?"

He replied, "You know very well that most Bible colleges and seminaries do not teach students to be Christlike disciples. When they come to me for training, I do not ask them to do things that I don't do; everywhere they go, I go with them.

"Everything I do is designed and planned carefully to make them count the cost. If they cannot count the cost, I do not want to spend three months just to find out that they will not make it. So, right from the start, I give them the chance to count the cost. Most of them go back.

"K.P.," he finished with his little smile, "this is not the first time this has happened. You have only just now come to know what has been happening here."

Needless to say, I was silent. There was nothing more to say. And after all of my indignant words, I did nothing to change what Paulose was doing.

Loving Jesus More Than Life

As he ministers each day in Rameswaram and the surrounding villages, Paulose has a team of over twenty believers who join with him.

During the civil war in Sri Lanka, hundreds of thousands of refugees fled to India each year—and

Rameswaram was one of the places where they arrived. The refugees were haggard and weary, half-dead from lack of food. They had barely escaped with their lives.

Each morning the gospel team would rise early to go to the seashore and count the number of refugees that had come in. Then they immediately went back to cook breakfast and tea for these people. After serving them food, the remainder of their day was full of ministry and outreach.

I do not know how many hours of sleep the team members got during those days of ministering to the refugees. But Paulose and his team labored seven days a week, for months on end.

One of the team members who worked alongside Paulose came from a middle-class family. At one point his family was quite upset with him because he chose not to marry.

Once again, I questioned Paulose. "Is it because you are brainwashing him with your radical way of living that this young man is wasting his whole life like this?" I asked.

"You ask him," Paulose replied. "I would be happy for him to get married—I would gladly help in any way. I am married, and I have six children of my own. Why don't you talk to him?"

So I did. The next time I saw this young man, I asked, "Is everything all right with you?"

"Yes, fine," he replied.

"What about your plans to get married?" I probed.

He said, "I want to be able to serve the Lord without being married."

I thought perhaps if I waited until I saw him the next time, he might be willing for me to help him find a wife (that's how we do it in India), but each time I asked, he firmly told me, "No."

Then it began to dawn on me how Paulose could build a team of people who were willing to live the grueling life-style that he chose and minister the gospel under very difficult circumstances. He never drew these people by compulsion or force. Rather, it was their willingness to die for the sake of the cross. Having counted the cost, they loved Jesus more than life itself.

A Principle of Emptiness

I am sure that Paulose's call from the Lord is unique, different from any other, and I know the same was true of the apostle Paul's life as well. But I want you to think seriously about what you have just read and what you are about to read.

As I pondered my conversations with Paulose, I realized that there was a principle here—a basic principle involving our walk with the Lord and our service to Him: *God wants us, as we live our life and ministry for Him, to stand on emptiness.*

What is emptiness? It is a void, a vacuum, total nothingness. It is like holding onto something that you cannot tangibly feel. Your eyes see nothing, but still you follow after.

Standing on emptiness means that we are stripped of not only tangible things but the intangible as well. Everything we are, everything in which we trusted— our expectations of acceptance, approval, security, importance, abilities and our rights—all are gone.

Many people around the world deliberately strip themselves of all material goods because they seek internal peace. In India, more than any other country, there are thousands who teach and practice asceticism. Buddha was a wealthy prince who left his wife and child. And for the rest of his life he wandered around the country meditating. That is how the whole religion of Buddhism began.

But this is not what I am talking about. What Buddha (and many others like him) did was only the self working to gain salvation. It begins with man and ends with man.

The Lord wants us to come to a place where nothing is there for us—except Himself. As Paul said, it is so that "the excellency of the power may be of God, and not of us" (2 Cor. 4:7). In other words, he is saying, "We are nothing. We are dying daily. There is nothing in us that we can acknowledge or about which we can say, 'I did that.'"

Jesus told the crowds, "Unless you love Me supremely—more than your father, your mother, your wife, your children, your brothers and your sisters, and even more than your own life—you cannot be my disciple" (see Luke 14:26).

The rich young ruler lacked only one thing to inherit eternal life. Jesus told him, "Sell all that thou hast, and distribute unto the poor, and thou shalt have treasure in heaven: and come, follow me" (Luke 18:22). This young man went away troubled, because he still loved his riches more than he did eternal life.

What we see throughout the Bible is God drawing His people to a place where they are suspended over empty space, where they operate out of faith and total dependency, where there is nothing tangible to cling to except God.

We Want Someone More Predictable

Do you remember when Israel wanted a king? They told Samuel, "Make us a king to judge us like all the nations" (1 Sam. 8:5). Have you ever thought why these people wanted someone to rule over them?

They wanted to be sure of what would happen tomorrow. They wanted to be confident that things would work out a certain way. They wanted that secure feeling of knowing the storehouses were full and that if something disastrous happened, a king would be there to take care of them. They wanted a king to be there to defend them with his army if need be. The Israelites only requested something that is a matter of normal, logical human life here on earth.

But what did God want from them? He told Samuel, "They have not rejected thee, but they have rejected me, that I should not reign over them" (1 Sam. 8:7). He told the people, "*I* am your King."

The Israelites were basically saying, "Now, God, this is not fair. Yes, You are our King, but You are so unpredictable! We fail You, and You say that You are not with us. We do something wrong, and You walk away. We go to fight, and we are killed. Later You tell us that it happened because we sinned, and that we had better repent. Couldn't You help us out when we're in a tight spot and tell us later about our sins?

"So please understand our feelings—and give us a king also."

You see, the Israelites were no different from all human beings—no different from us.

What did God want? He wanted them to be in a place where they were standing on emptiness. He wanted them to reach a point where they could say, "We don't know about tomorrow, but that doesn't matter, because the Lord is our tomorrow. He is all that we need." The Lord wanted them to give up everything that was reasonable, right and logical from their point of view.

In the end, of course, God gave them a king; but not before He warned them that the king would take their sons and daughters, their fields and vineyards, their donkeys and sheep—and they would be his servants.

Strength from Numbers

Go with me to another passage, 2 Samuel 24, where David commanded Joab, his captain, to take a census of the army of Israel. Joab protested, "God is the one who has given you the people—it doesn't matter how many there are."

We are told that "the king's word prevailed against Joab" (2 Sam. 24:4). Do you remember what ultimately happened? Seventy-thousand men were wiped out as a result of David's disobedience to God.

This does not seem reasonable to our logical minds. After all, David was the king. He had every right to know what he had in terms of strength just in case another army rose up against Israel. It's the most reasonable, logical thing to take an inventory.

But David forgot the times when he was a young boy, watching sheep, and he had to face wild animals. He forgot about the time he confronted Goliath. Who gave David the victories then? He did not have many people to count on his side then. All he had was God. God was all he needed.

It was not the people who were the problem in this story. It was David's inner attitude. David had come to a place in his life where he no longer wanted to stand on emptiness. He wanted certainty and knowledge. And ultimately his pride led to terrible destruction.

As Long as He Sought the Lord

Uzziah was one of the kings of Judah who followed the Lord, and he began his reign at the age of sixteen. As you read 1 Chronicles 26, you will find that

Uzziah accomplished an incredible number of tasks while he was king.

"He did that which was right in the sight of the LORD ... and as long as he sought the LORD, God made him to prosper" (2 Chron. 26:4-5). Verse 7 says, "God helped him." Do you realize that we are reading about a sixteen-year-old boy in this passage?

If you continue reading, you will see that Uzziah's life did not end as well as it had begun. Verse 16 says, "But when he was strong, his heart was lifted up to his destruction."

Suddenly, Uzziah was a self-contained, self-made man. He was no longer an unsure, awkward child of sixteen. He knew his way around. He had a reputation. He could negotiate and wheel and deal. Now he had an air of dignity about him, and he knew correct protocol for every situation.

Do you see what can happen when you trust in your own strength? Your heart becomes lifted up to your own destruction. It is an attitude of the heart for which we must continually be on guard, lest we become deceived to think we have it made.

No Confidence in the Flesh

God promised Abraham from the very beginning that He would produce out of him a great nation; but He deliberately waited to fulfill that promise until it seemed impossible to Abraham.

Finally Abraham came to the place where he could say, "Lord, just look at me. I am an old, wrinkled man. There is nothing left in my body that could produce a child. It is as good as dead. And look at Sarah—she is an old woman. Her ability to bear children ceased long ago. Lord, I am one hundred and she is ninety—and You still say we are going to have a child!"

God waited until Abraham was standing on his own emptiness—totally dependent on God. Abraham and Sarah knew that it would have to be an act of God if they were to still have a child. Then God was able to work (see Gen. 21).

We Want an Agenda

When God led the children of Israel out of Egypt, He miraculously spared their oldest sons in the final plague, He opened the Red Sea for them to walk through on dry ground, and He provided food and water for them each step of the way.

What do we see happening in the camp, though? They began to grumble and complain because God would not work on their schedule. They wanted an agenda—perhaps something like this: "Tomorrow we will have breakfast, lunch and dinner at these times. The first day we will have beef, the next day chicken and the following day fish. After three months, we will have a change of clothing and shoes. When we reach that certain spot, we will have water."

Their expectations were logical and reasonable. But God did not lead them in that matter, did He? He told them, "When the cloud moves, you move. When the cloud stops, you stop" (see Ex. 40:36-38).

What was God trying to do? He wanted the children of Israel to stand on emptiness. He desired for their hearts to be fully focused on Him, not on where they would go or what they would eat the next day.

Too Many People

Gideon had thirty-two hundred warriors with him when he first planned to war against the Midianites. But the Lord told him, "The people that are with thee are too many for me to give the Midianites into their hands, lest Israel vaunt themselves against me, saying, Mine own hand hath saved me" (Judg. 7:2).

Twice the Lord reduced the number of the army until there were only three hundred men left.

Gideon must have been thinking, *What? Too many? These Midianites are rough, Lord. Their army is without number—they are like grasshoppers camped out there in the valley. We need all the people we can get.*

The Lord told Gideon to choose the men who lapped the water by putting their hand to their mouth. There were only three hundred who did so. These men were not stupid—they knew the enemy they were about to fight. They knew very well it was impossible to win. Yet they were willing to go into battle, regardless of the outcome.

These men were willing to stand on emptiness. They realized that the war did not depend on them but that God would fight for them. They did not have to trust in themselves at all—it was totally up to Him.

This was a major test that the Lord led these men through, and what was its purpose? To weed out those who did not put their trust wholly in the Lord. Finally He found a handful of people who recognized the principle of standing on emptiness.

I Know That My Redeemer Lives

The story of Job is another fascinating example. The Lord said to Satan, "Hast thou considered my servant Job, that there is none like him in the earth, a perfect and an upright man, one that feareth God, and escheweth evil?" (Job 1:8).

Satan's reply to the Lord went something like this: "You say he is righteous and godly. But I tell You

179

what—You let me have him for a little while, and I'll tell You if he really means business with You."

What did Satan do to Job? He stripped him of everything. Job lost his children, his house, his land, his herds—everything. Finally Job found himself in a heap of ashes, his body covered with boils, scraping himself with a piece of pottery.

Well, Job might have said to himself, *at least I still have my wife to stand by me. She has lived with me, slept with me, borne my children for so many years. She knows my thoughts, she sees my life. She will understand.*

Then his wife turned to him and said, "Why are you suffering like this? Curse God so you can at least die and get out of your misery."

Well, at least I have my friends to support me, Job may have thought. *Even if all is lost, even if I am sick for many years to come, they are here. They cannot heal me or do anything to change my situation, but at least they understand me. At least they can offer me some inner courage to help me through these struggles.*

His friends arrived, and upon hearing about Job's difficulties, spent nearly the rest of the book misunderstanding him and accusing him. He could hardly open his mouth before they would use what he said against him.

Finally, despite all of the accusations mounted against him, what does Job say? "I know that my redeemer liveth" (Job 19:25).

"Everything I had is now gone. It's all right. All I have is total emptiness to stand on, but that's okay. I know that there is something more real than all of this."

In the end Job came through the test, pure and approved.

Are You Going to Leave Me Too?

At certain points in our walk with the Lord, we all become discouraged and demotivated. We want to quit. We want to run away. Many men in the Bible—Moses, Elijah, Jonah, David—felt the same way.

Paul said in 2 Corinthians 1:8 that he had "despaired even of life." Later he wrote to Timothy, saying that all in Asia had forsaken him (see 2 Tim. 4:16). Discouragement is part of what we face in our walk with the Lord.

Some think Jesus had only twelve disciples, but if you read the gospels you will find that He had many more than that. At one point in His ministry, at least eighty-two men followed Jesus.

Everything was going wonderfully for them. They were fed and taken care of, they saw spectacular miracles being performed, thousands were coming to see Jesus and lives were being touched. It was a great life!

One day Jesus took them all aside and said, "I want to tell you the other side of the story." They eagerly perked up their ears to what He had to say.

And then Jesus told them, "I am going to die."

This was totally new information for them. As He explained more about His suffering and coming death on the cross, seventy disciples just walked away (see John 6). They couldn't handle His words and the lifestyle He exampled before them.

Jesus turned to the others and said, "Are you going to leave Me too?"

Then Peter replied, "Lord, where would we go? You have the words of eternal life."

One group of people saw the cross as a means of loss, discouragement and death. Only a few saw the life and the hope that the cross had to offer.

181

It will always be like this in following the Lord. A huge crowd may start out, just as in a marathon; but in the end only a few survive. We are told to run in such a way that we will win (see 1 Cor. 9:24).

Unprofitable Servants

Jesus told a parable in Luke 17 of a servant who worked all day in the fields, plowing and feeding cattle. At the end of the day his master arrived home. The servant then prepared his master's supper and waited on him while he ate. Afterward the servant cleaned up; finally, late into the evening, he ate his own supper.

What does Jesus say this servant's response—and ours—is to be?

"After all that I have done for you, Master, I am still an unprofitable servant. There is nothing that I am or that I have done which gives me even one square inch to stand on and say, 'I have done it. I paid the price.'"

This is where the Lord wants us to be.

You may ask me all sorts of questions: "Brother K.P., how can we be sure that we'll be able to accomplish this task of world evangelism? It's going to take a lot of work—can we handle it? Don't you think your plan is a little outrageous?"

All I can say is that the Lord is with us. Have you seen how the wind comes and carries off the dry leaves from beneath a tree? That is the best way for me to explain what I mean. Let the wind of the Lord blow us away and carry us wherever He wishes.

"And then what?" you may ask. "That makes no sense; we need to know more."

I do not know. I don't know where the Lord will have me go tomorrow or next year. All I know is that I am standing on emptiness. I am declaring total dependence upon the Lord. I have nothing in myself that I can cling to. There is nothing in my own strength that will carry me.

It is He who leads me, whether that means having everything or nothing. All that matters is Him.

Chapter 14

STRIPPING AWAY OUR
SECRET LONGINGS

I was sitting at my desk, working on correspondence and phone contacts, when a knock came at the door. "Come in," I called.

Dave, our computer department manager, poked his head in the door. "Brother K.P., I have some information here I think you would like to see." We were in the process of making a decision on a much-needed computer system for our headquarters in Texas. *This must be another report we need for the purchase,* I thought.

As I read through the figures and dates which plotted our growth in the near future, I became excited. *Wow*! I said to myself, *this is fantastic! We are doing really well.* My mind started to project into the next five to ten years, and I imagined to myself, *We are most certainly going to become one of the important ministries in the days to come*!

After Dave left, the Lord began to speak seriously to my heart: "What is this ministry really all about? Are these plans what you are setting your hopes on? Are you standing on your own dreams and schemes, or are you standing on emptiness?"

I realized what I had just done. For a few moments I had forgotten that it was the Lord who had brought us to the place where we were today. It was nothing we could have done—and yet, when I saw that report plotting our estimated growth, I secretly longed for more recognition, more acceptance.

As believers who are serving the Lord with a serious, sober-minded commitment, let us guard our hearts from entertaining thoughts like, *Now we have made it based on our past actions*, or *We can surely do it ourselves—all we need is some more genius planning.* I can tell you from personal experience—it is dangerous to fall into this trap!

Just before the children of Israel were about to pass over the Jordan River into the promised land, God issued them a very solemn warning:

"Beware that thou forget not the LORD thy God, in not keeping his commandments, and his judgments, and his statutes, which I command thee this day:

"Lest when thou hast eaten and art full, and hast built goodly houses ... and when thy herds and thy flocks multiply, and thy silver and thy gold is multiplied, and all that thou hast is multiplied; then thine heart be lifted up and thou forget the LORD thy God, which brought thee forth out of the land of Egypt, from the house of bondage ... and thou say in thine heart, My power and the might of mine hand hath gotten me this wealth.

"But thou shalt remember the LORD thy God: for *it is he that giveth thee power* ...

"And it shall be, if thou do at all forget the LORD thy God, and walk after other gods, and serve them, and worship them, I testify against you this day that ye shall surely perish" (Deut. 8:11-14;17-19).

The attitude of our heart should be one of prayerfully looking to the Lord, continuously saying, "Lord, as far as my life is concerned—my future, my plans, my ideas, my dreams, my hopes—there is nothing I could stand on to say I could make it work. Lord, You have the total freedom to lead me where You wish."

We need to identify and then strip away that secret longing we have within us for reputation, acceptance, security and the approval of others. Jesus laid all of this down when He went outside of the city, out of the gate, bearing the shame of the cross. We are called to follow Him: "Let us go forth therefore unto him without the camp, bearing his reproach" (Heb. 13:13).

Live or Die—Fine

In 1966 I joined Operation Mobilization and began eight years of intensive gospel outreach. I came as a sixteen-year-old boy, my skinny legs poking out through my shorts, barely having any knowledge of any language other than my native tongue. I didn't know much about anything—but I was certain of the Lord's calling on my life.

Each year the leadership of OM India would gather the entire force of missionaries together—around three to four hundred of us—for a conference. New strategies were planned, and we were challenged, refreshed and encouraged.

It was a typical occurrence during those days for one of the leaders to stand up in front of all of us and say, "Brothers and sisters, we need to pray—we have

187

no more food." I was hungry—and so I prayed! It was wonderful to see how the Lord answered our prayers, meeting all our needs.

After the conference was over, we were divided up into teams of about eight or nine members. Each team was assigned an area of India. We had a leader and an old, beat-up truck to carry literature. We were given a few dollars for food, our truck was filled with tracts and gospel literature—and off we went. There we were, sitting on crates in the back of the truck, swerving and bouncing around on thousands of miles of Indian roads.

We would put diesel in the truck and drive as far as we could. By that time our money had run out as well. Our leader would tell us, "Let's pray, and then we'll go and sell our gospel literature." By the afternoon we would have enough money from the sale of our literature to buy a few *chappatis* (tortilla-like breads) for each of us, as well as fill up the truck with more diesel. Our leader would say, "All right, one hour of rest, and then we'll be going again." Day in and day out, that is how we lived.

Some of the local churches wouldn't even receive our teams because they perceived us to be real fanatics. "If these OM people come to our place, they will make us feel as though we are going to hell. We don't want their preaching," they would say.

We would sleep on the side of the road, under the truck. One night it rained so hard that even the roadside was filled with a swirling, muddy flood. Shivering like rats, we all crawled into the back of the truck, where we hardly found even a place to sit. Bright and early the next morning, we would move on.

Several years went by, and I became a team leader. One day in North India I was called upon to preach in a meeting. At that point in my life I owned two shirts, two pairs of pants and a pair of sneakers.

In the wintertime North India is a very cold place, and today was no exception. The electricity had gone out that day, so all the windows were open for light. The winter wind blew mercilessly through the building, and I was freezing. As I stood there in my thin shirt, holding my Bible, everyone waited expectantly. They were all wearing thick, woolen blankets and coats. I shivered. My knees were knocking together, and my teeth were chattering so hard I could no longer speak.

"Lord," I said in my heart, "I believe I am doing what You told me to do, but I cannot even open my mouth, much less talk. I want to talk to these people about You, but I can't. Please help me."

Suddenly I felt as if there was a wall of fire around me. Instantly I was warm! The Lord had answered my prayer. That day I preached on hell—and a few were saved at the end of my message!

The strange thing about this miracle was that I was only warm during the time I preached. As soon as I finished I began to shiver and chatter once again.

All those years I was with this gospel team, we literally lived out some of the passages in the New Testament. We were continually faced with loss, persecution, beatings and stonings. We never even worried about whether we would live or die. All we had was one thought in our hearts: *These people don't know the Lord. Live or die—fine. We will preach the gospel. If we are killed, praise the Lord—heaven is a better place anyway.*

Please don't misunderstand me—I am not saying you have to endure such things to prove your spirituality.

What I am saying is this: We were asked to live and walk on emptiness. We had basically nothing in this world. All we could do was cling to Him, because there was no one and nothing else there.

I am not advocating that you be compelled by guilt or obligation to part with your material goods. But I cannot say strongly enough how vitally important it is to come to the place where you have nothing else to depend on except the Lord.

No Product of the Flesh

The apostle Paul was obviously an intelligent man. He lists his résumé for us in Philippians 3. He was well educated and "touching the righteousness which is in the law, blameless" (Phil. 3:6).

But he goes on to tell us, "All those things that I would consider benefits to me—my strength, my abilities, my influence, everything I have—I have made a decision to count it as dung. Trash. Rubbish. Every day I start from zero, I work from zero, I walk with zero. And this is how I have chosen to live" (see Phil. 3:8).

Toward the end of his life, when he knew his enemies were waiting for him, he said, "All I know is this—I don't love my life very much. I don't take it seriously, and I don't cling to it. So whether I live or die, it doesn't really matter" (see Acts 20:22-25). There was nothing he was standing on that he was afraid of falling from; there was nothing he was clinging to that he was afraid of losing.

Plans and strategies are not wrong, but we must realize we don't even come close to knowing all the answers. We must allow Him to do what He wants to do with our lives. And where we may have some strength that we can use, let us come to terms with ourselves and say honestly to the Lord, "Fine, Lord, I have the strength, I acknowledge it. I know that I am strong in this particular area, but I also know that this is not what You desire."

When all is said and done, when history is sealed up and time runs out, God is going to make sure that nothing that is a product of the flesh will last for eternity. He has never accepted a work of our own flesh, and He never will, however good it might look in our sight. Nothing, not even our turning the world upside down or preaching thousands of sermons, will enter into eternity if it has been a product of our flesh. God will make sure that anything lasting for eternity will be all of Him and Him alone. And only those who stand on emptiness, who cling to nothingness, will be able to accomplish that.

Willing to Die

On a past trip to India, a letter arrived for me while I was there. It was certified, and I had to sign for it. When I opened the envelope, I found a letter wrapped around several pieces of Bible portions. The portions were half-burned, and when I pulled them out, the edges were charred. A little ash remained in the envelope.

As I unfolded the letter and began to read it, I slowly sat down. Addressed to me, it was from one of the leaders of a militant Hindu movement.

The letter described all of the things I was involved in—my radio program, supporting missionaries, holding prayer meetings—everything. The list was intended to convince me that I was being watched closely. "We are sending you this letter as a warning," the man wrote. "Unless you stop these activities, you will not be alive many more days or months." It was signed by this leader—in blood.

Later I began to think about this letter again, and about Gospel for Asia. *What are we doing in this ministry*? I asked myself. *What are we creating on the*

191

mission field? What type of workers and leaders are we producing? What is the direction we are heading? What kind of life are we challenging people to live?

The Lord strongly impressed this upon my heart: We must do everything we can to help our people come to the place where they are willing to be martyred for the gospel. They must arrive at the point where they have nothing left to cling to but the Lord. They must stand on total emptiness. If they live or if they die, it doesn't matter.

Before he was saved, Isaac was a very devout Hindu. To please his gods, he would spend a month or two preparing himself for a special ceremony. During this time he would avoid certain foods, according to the likes or dislikes of the demon gods he worshiped, who then would come to possess Isaac's body. Isaac would offer the blood of nearly sixty chickens to these deities.

Then, as the time drew nearer, he would sit and chant while beating a drum. Suddenly he would go into a trance, and then the ceremony would begin. Because of the power of the demons who possessed him, Isaac was able to pierce his cheeks with arrows, walk on fire and put hooks through the muscles of his back to pull an idol on a cart.

When Isaac found Jesus, he forsook his gods and was delivered from all demonic possession. Now Isaac travels to different areas as an evangelist, sharing the gospel and winning souls to Jesus. But not without a price.

A short while ago Isaac went to a nearby village to preach and share his testimony. While he was still speaking, a gang of people grabbed him and told him, "Just as you used to cut the chickens' throats and shed their blood, we will now cut you and shed your blood!"

They dragged him away from the village to a heavily wooded area and beat him severely. Then his persecutors tied him to a tree, his hands pulled backward around the trunk, and left to call more people to kill him. The tree had been carefully selected, for it was covered with fierce, biting ants.

The ants crawled all over his body, biting him repeatedly. Isaac was in terrible pain, and he lapsed in and out of consciousness.

Then, in the haze of his agony, he saw an old woman, perhaps eighty years old, standing in front of him. She untied him and told him, "You must leave here quickly." He did as he was told immediately, and as he was leaving, he looked back for the old lady. There was no one there—she had vanished! Isaac realized that God had provided a way for his escape.

One week after the incident, Isaac came to a local pastor's conference and shared his testimony. Many of the pastors were challenged and encouraged to hear of his faith in the Lord and his willingness to lay down his life. Isaac continues to travel to nearby villages and preach the gospel.

More Like Jesus

How about you? Have you stripped yourself of those secret longings deep within your heart for recognition, security and acceptance?

Is there something the Lord has asked you to do, but you have put it off because you feel you will lose control of the situation?

What has hindered you from giving unselfishly to reach the lost in our generation?

Can you honestly say that this world is not your home, and that you are simply passing through?

If someone were to point a gun at you and say,

"Deny Christ or I will kill you," what would your response be? Can you say as Paul did, "neither count I my life dear unto myself"? (Acts 20:24).

Is your prayer life proof of your total dependence upon the Lord? Do you ask the Lord to show you His plans, or do you just ask Him to bless your own agenda?

The days before us will not be easy ones—neither for our brothers and sisters on the mission field, nor for believers in the West. I foresee major attacks, opposition and even martyrdom for many of our missionaries.

But those who will stand are the ones who have nothing to cling to, because if there was something left in their lives that they counted dear, they would have run off in fear.

I cannot write any words that will make you something you are not. All I can do is share examples and illustrations. God has to do the work within you, developing your heart and your attitude.

The most vital thing for all of us is that we become more like Jesus. We are all growing and changing in our walk with the Lord, and there will always be opportunities to live out what He has taught us.

Chapter 15

JUST A HANDFUL OF DUST

After returning from a trip to the mission field, I lay awake in bed, hours before my alarm clock was set to go off. It usually happens this way—jet lag lingers for about a week before my new schedule sets in.

I decided to get up and get dressed anyway and write that one letter that kept circulating in my mind.

I had been thinking of writing a lengthy letter to the GFA leaders who served in the countries where we supported native missionaries. They were scattered over ten nations, hard at work in the service of the Lord, reaching the unreached of their land with the gospel. I knew that each leader was so heavily involved in his own work that it was virtually impossible for him to know what or how any other leaders were doing.

I wanted to share with them an overall picture of the work. I wanted them to be encouraged that they were not alone in the task God had given them to do. I wanted to challenge them to pray for the leaders in other countries and for their ministries as well.

I sat at my desk and made a list of all I wanted to share with these leaders. As I wrote down what the Lord had done for us in the past year, my list grew longer and longer. It was obvious I would eventually have to shorten my letter, but still I was amazed to think about each event, orchestrated by the hand of God, that took place over one year's time.

Reports from the field told me, "Fifty thousand people came to the Lord over the past two months from watching the film of Jesus.... We have just completed construction of the one hundredth church building in North India among the tribal converts.... Three hundred bicycles were given to native missionaries in the past four months.... We have just placed an order for another one hundred film projectors, and they will be sent out in a few weeks' time to be used on the field."

I knew that a massive wave of persecution had recently broken out in various parts of Asia. Many believers' houses were set on fire and many brothers and sisters were beaten severely because of the large numbers of people who were coming to the Lord.

One leader told me, "This past year we had a goal to enlist at least one hundred missionaries to go to the unreached areas. We have already passed that mark."

I knew of thousands of missionaries who were ready and willing to head out to remote, pioneer areas; all they needed was training and support.

As I sat there, I wrote down answer to prayer after answer to prayer. It was almost too much to believe. Nearly everything we'd set our hands to do had been accomplished.

The First Dollar Bill

In the midst of my amazement and rejoicing, my heart was sobered as I remembered David's prayer in Psalm 19: "Keep back thy servant also from presumptuous sins; let them not have dominion over me" (Ps. 19:13). One of my greatest fears is that someday I will take the goodness of the Lord for granted. That's the purpose of this chapter—to show that nothing we do for the Lord can ever come from our own strength.

Not too long ago, Margaret, our bookkeeper for our Texas office, brought me an envelope and showed me what was inside. Four dollar bills—very special ones. I had written on each of them in red. I had given them to her to keep, but I myself had forgotten why they were there until she brought them out that day.

A few years ago Gisela and I and Terry, another member of our staff, sat around the dinner table and reminisced about the years we each spent with Operation Mobilization. We remembered "the good old days" when we walked from village to village, and then how our ministry dramatically changed when we were able to use a truck or a van to get from place to place. All of a sudden we were able to really move out, full steam ahead, penetrating the unreached areas with the gospel.

How wonderful it would be, we thought, if we could purchase vehicles for our native missionaries now and equip them with gospel literature, a generator, a projector and a film on the life of Christ. Then we could send teams to remote, unreached areas to spread the gospel. At that time, purchasing and equipping even one van was a major ordeal. At $12,000 each, we did not come by them easily. The more we talked, however, the more convinced I became that van teams could prove to be a major force in reaching our generation for Christ.

As we sat there, I took out a dollar bill from my wallet and wrote on it in big red letters, "The first dollar down payment, by faith, toward the purchase of 100 vehicles." Then I took another out and wrote, "The first dollar down payment for projectors," and so on until there were four dollar bills sitting there, representing our faith in the Lord to provide the various needs we had on the mission field.

To date, we have been able to provide enough funds to purchase over seventy vans and equip them to reach pioneer areas that have never had a gospel witness! This means that on each van team, five missionaries are able to travel all over India, going to thousands of villages and sharing the love of Jesus with as many as they are able. For the majority of those simple village people, it will be the first time in their lives that they have ever heard the name of Jesus.

When I saw those four dollar bills in the envelope, I was reminded again that nothing we had done had made this come to pass. It was God and God alone who did it. And I was reminded again of the importance of giving Him the glory for all these wonderful things that were happening.

The Most Important Thing

After I finished my list of what the Lord had done, I began to look ahead to the new year before us. Tremendous opportunities awaited us. Time was short, and I knew we had to keep pressing on to win our generation.

I felt strongly that the Lord was calling us to expand our work to other countries in Southeast Asia. We needed to think about putting out millions of pieces of gospel literature in as many languages as possible. Two thousand missionaries were ready to receive support and begin full-time service on the mission field. I longed to see at least three or four daily radio broadcasts in different languages. There was a tremendous need to set up at least half a dozen Bible correspondence course schools where there would be someone to follow up on the thousands who wrote in with questions, wanting to learn more about the gospel.

There was so much to do. Our opportunities looked unlimited. And I was convinced that with every need the Lord was going to provide the finances and the staff to handle the growth that would come.

But beyond the pull of this challenge to spread the gospel into Third World nations, I knew that something was far more important.

Yes, world evangelism was important. But the greatest and most important thing I needed to keep in mind was that we were *totally dependent upon the Lord.*

As Little Children

You see, if we are not completely looking to the Lord to meet all of our needs, we begin to look to ourselves to make things happen. And ultimately only disaster can come of that.

I remember the days when we prayed for forty dollars so we could buy postage stamps! I remember calling all over the place trying to arrange even one meeting.

Something wonderful happens in our lives when we regard ourselves as helplessly dependent upon the Lord.

In our hearts and attitudes, we must always remain as little children before Him. If there is anything we have, anything that we are allowed to accomplish, it is because of the Lord and His grace.

The secret of the Lord's blessing upon any work, large or small, is that all of the glory goes to Him.

But how is this possible for humans like us, who live in flesh-and-blood bodies that naturally strive for personal praise whenever possible? Look at Psalm 103:14: "For he knoweth our frame, he remembereth that we are dust." I am assured by this verse that the Lord knows the kind of stuff I am made of.

The question is, Am *I* able to remember this? *Do I daily recognize that all I am made of is a little handful of dust?*

The Lord rescues us so many times from our tendency to cease depending upon Him. In His mercy He often keeps us from doing things in our own flesh instead of in His strength.

Give Us a Chance, and We'll Go Astray

In Deuteronomy 31, just before Moses' death, God called Moses and Joshua to present themselves before Him in the tabernacle. What did God tell them?

"Behold, [Moses,] thou shalt sleep with thy fathers; and this people will rise up, and go a whoring after the gods of the strangers of the land, whither they go to be among them, and will forsake me, and break my covenant which I have made with them. Then my anger shall be kindled against them in that day, and I will forsake them, and I will hide my face from them ..." (Deut. 31:16-17).

We are like sheep. Give us a chance, and we'll go astray. We are no different in our human nature than the children of Israel.

Take a look around you at the people and the ministries you know of whom God has called to do His heart's desire. I am sad to say that you will most often find that flesh has gotten in the way. People become arrogant and take the glory for themselves.

What Will It Take?

In a country like India, I foresee that sometime in the near future many thousands will be killed for their faith. All the signs are pointing to this.

What will it take to live in times like these? Not Bible knowledge, great zeal, impeccable philosophy, missions conferences, computer printouts or group investigations. It will take people who are willing to say, "I came to this place with a one-way ticket. I am here to live and die. You can kill me if you want, but I am here to preach the gospel. My life no longer belongs to me—I have given it as a sacrifice."

If the Lord is going to use someone for His purposes, He often has to strip away their dependence on intelligence, education, abilities and their strengths before He can truly use them. He has to make them nothing before He can build them back up again for His service.

It is much easier for God to build something significant through a person's life if he or she has completely surrendered to the Lord. This is a tested and proven fact throughout the Bible and on the mission field today as well.

Serving Our Generation

We read this about one man of God: "David, after he had *served his own generation* by the will of God, fell on sleep, and was laid unto his fathers" (Acts 13:36). Our desire ought not be to put down roots and secure something for the future. The Lord is the One who calls people. He is the One who makes things happen. He is the One who calls the shots.

In Gospel for Asia, it has been wonderfully refreshing to see over the years how God has carried us along. Some of the things we carefully planned never took place. Some things that we never expected happened in a mighty way. And we have known beyond a shadow of a doubt that God has done these things.

As believers we need to continually acknowledge this in our own hearts. After doing all the things that we know we should do, we have not gained one credit or one mark for what we have done. It is all because of the Lord.

I pray that we would no longer trust in our own understanding, nor even live for our cause. You see, the cause is important—but the Lord is more important than anything else.

One of the most wonderful things about being in this position is that it is the safest place to be. No matter whether we are in the midst of the severest battle, the greatest agony—we know that the Lord is with us! Whatever you do, there is the potential that much more can happen simply because the Lord is doing it and not you.

Chapter 16

CHANGING LIVES ON OUR KNEES

I remember a point in my life when I realized I needed to pray more. An hour seemed like a good place to start.

Early the next morning I woke up, and after making sure I was awake, I knelt by the side of my bed and started to pray. I poured out my heart to the Lord. I prayed about everything I could think of. When I had finished, I figured at least forty-five minutes had gone by, if not the whole hour.

I looked at my clock. I had prayed for only four minutes! Now what was I going to do? I had prayed about everything I knew. What would I do for the next fifty-six minutes?

Have you ever felt the way I did? Suddenly, prayer wasn't as simple as it seemed.

Alone with God

Unless we are praying and spending time with the Lord, we cannot understand what it means to follow Christ. We are so often deceived into thinking that a few good choruses and hymns, a dynamic sermon and an outstanding church program are where it's at. But we are wrong.

One of God's highest agendas throughout the Bible is to get His people to the place where they are all alone. Jacob ran from God for twenty years or more before God met him alone. Only then could He make him Israel.

You see, when it is just God and you, you come face to face with yourself—and your sins. With everyone else, you can argue these things away, or you can smile and cover it up. But when you are all alone before God, you have to face yourself. And only then can cleansing and purification take place. When you spend time alone with the Lord, reality sets in. You can no longer be a phony.

I cannot stress enough how vital it is to develop a consistent prayer life. Otherwise your walk with the Lord will lack reality and credibility.

Going into Battle

But this is only the first step in God's agenda for your life. He also wants to make you aware of the more than two billion lives who are still unreached with the gospel. Each one is created in the image of God, with an eternal soul. Yet they are bound in chains of sin, heading toward hell, not knowing there is a name to call upon for salvation. God is searching for those who will stand in the gap on their behalf and intercede for their souls.

I am not talking about a little phrase you add to your prayer at the dinner table: "Lord, please bless our food and our family—and save the heathens in Africa."

No—I am talking about entering an incredible spiritual battle. What I mean is a conscious, deliberate choice to wage warfare against the powers of darkness for the release of souls who have no one else to fight for their deliverance.

Paul exhorts us to pray in Ephesians 6—"For we wrestle not against flesh and blood, but against principalities, against powers, against the rulers of the darkness of this world, against spiritual wickedness in high places.... Praying always with all prayer and supplication in the Spirit, and watching thereunto with all perseverance and supplication for all saints" (Eph. 6:12,18).

We face tremendous opportunities today on the mission field. People's hearts are open to receive the gospel, and we are able to send workers into the most unreached areas.

However, at the same time we face a great increase in opposition and persecution on the mission field. We also face self-centeredness and misunderstandings within the body of Christ, which often hinder the willingness of the church to give to missions.

We need to unite together to pray against the powers of darkness. We will not see things happen any other way. Breakthroughs will come on our knees, not by sitting and wishing for them to happen.

The Hardest—and the Easiest

Prayer is one of the most difficult jobs you will ever undertake—but it is the weapon of warfare that guarantees victory.

You will also ultimately discover that prayer is the quickest way to get anything done. What would otherwise take fifty years of struggle can be accomplished in five—if the battles are first won in prayer. I have seen this happen over and over again on the front lines of the mission field.

When you read about the lives of the New Testament Christians, you will find that when they were threatened or harassed, when they faced struggles and problems—they immediately met for prayer. And the book of Acts records this about their prayer meeting: "And when they had prayed, the place was shaken where they were assembled together; and they were all filled with the Holy Ghost, and they spake the word of God with boldness" (Acts 4:31).

These people rooted their every action in prayer. They were filled with power to do the impossible, and they radically impacted their community. These people were unlearned and uneducated. They had no special training. But everyone knew they had spent time with Jesus (see Acts 4:13).

Moving the Hand of God

Do you ever say things to yourself like this?

I'm so tired of the way my husband lives his life. I thought all these years that he was an honest man, but now I've found out that his private life is not so wonderful.

I'm frustrated with my wife's unwillingness to commit her life to the cause of the Lord's kingdom. I wish she wouldn't resist my efforts to pray and give to the Lord. I wish things would be different.

I'm tired of trying to witness to my coworker. All he does is make fun of my faith, and he seems to deliberately try to trap me or test me. I wish he would just change or leave.

What is your next step? Do you run out for the newest self-help booklet that will tell you how to make it work?

Throughout the Bible, there was one thing that moved the hand of Almighty God—and that was prayer.

On many occasions Jesus spent an entire night in prayer, often after a day of hard work. The next day He would go out and minister to people in the power of the Spirit. That strength, that dynamite-type power that flowed through Him was a direct result of His contact with the Father.

When was the last time you considered the implications of what serious prayer would do in your life?

Staying in Touch

You may say, "You're joking, right? Me—pray for an hour, a few days or a few weeks? Are you kidding?"

But, you see, God is in the business of making His children into the likeness of His Son. Romans 8:29 says, "For whom he did foreknow, he also did predestinate to be conformed to the image of his Son." But He cannot do this forming in us until He has some time with us.

When you have truly given your life to the Lord, it no longer belongs to you. You have died to your self. Now Jesus wants to live His life through you. Now you can take every concern straight to Him. "Jesus, I need to talk to this person about You. I don't know what to say, but I want to share with him. Could You please tell me what I must do?"

You see how simple it becomes when you are in tune with Him? You will find yourself just like the man who dug deep and anchored the foundation for his house upon bedrock. No matter what circumstances may bluster your way, you are not moved. You are solid because you are anchored to the Rock.

What happens if you fail to lay that foundation? You may have the most attractive house in the neighborhood—but if serious winds and rains come, it will suddenly be gone in a moment. "What happened?" the neighbors ask each other. "That fool," they will say. "He built his house with no foundation!"

Please don't misunderstand me—even if you have an inconsistent prayer life and you cry out to the Lord, He is merciful and will hear you. But if you develop a habit of praying and spending time with the Lord, you will realize how precious that cord of communication is.

You see, getting to know Jesus and loving Him is not a one-day thing. The more you know Him, the more you will love Him. And the more you love Him, the more your entire life will be revolutionized. But this only happens when you take the time to practice the presence of the Lord. It happens through prayer.

Changing the Course of History

Do you realize that some of the history-changing revivals took place, not through a massive effort of hundreds of people, but because a small handful of people prayed and fasted? Whole nations have been changed because three, four or five people were willing to get on their knees before the living God.

I know of a community in India where over 60 percent of the people came to Jesus Christ because a group of men prayed and fasted for two weeks before they would open their mouths to utter one word in the village. Prayer is what changes people, circumstances, nations and even history.

You may say, "But I am such a weak thing when it comes to prayer. I am not a mighty, spiritual man or woman. What can I do?"

I tell you this: When you are weak, when you stumble and fall—the cross of Christ becomes powerful! Jesus has told us, "My strength is made perfect in weakness" (2 Cor. 12:9).

The men and the women of God whose stories are recorded in the Bible are people who changed their circumstances. So many wait instead for their circumstances to change. "I'll be able to really do something for God when my ship comes in." Did you send a ship out? You can't guarantee whether one will come in or not!

You may say, "Well, I'll fast and pray for Tibet and for India when I have a little more physical strength.... I am going to sell out everything to serve the Lord after my retirement.... When my problems at home are solved, then I can focus on doing more.... I will think about ministry after I get married...."

How can you be a revolutionary with this attitude? Realize that you are able, by God's grace, to change your circumstances! God has given you this power, this treasure. But you do not realize what you have. You are not using what you have been given. Why not? Because the key to knowing your weapon is prayer— "praying always," says Ephesians 6:18. If you do not have a consistent prayer life, you cannot know the resources He has given you already.

More Praying Than Planning

As a ministry, Gospel for Asia is a fairly young organization—at the time of this writing we are close to the fifteen-year mark. But wherever I go I have people ask me the secret to our growth. One

209

organization even sent a delegate to our Dallas office to find out what was behind our growth.

I walked with the man through our office, and we talked. "Tell me, Brother K.P.," he said, "which agency does your fund raising?"

"We have no agency," I replied, "although we are not against them. Some agencies are made up of godly people called by the Lord to help build His kingdom."

"Well, then, what do you have?" He was a little confused.

I tried to explain. "Brother, at the very beginning of our ministry, we started a Tuesday evening prayer meeting that has been going on ever since. We meet from seven until nine every Tuesday night. Our office staff arrives half an hour early three mornings a week to pray before the day begins. And on the first Friday of each month we meet for all-night prayer, which lasts until three or four in the morning.

"We spend more time praying than planning. We simply pray for everything that happens. If we have a need for something, we just pray."

I'm not throwing out logical thought entirely. We *need* planning and budgeting; we need to have the best brainstorming sessions in order to learn how we can share the message more effectively. Nevertheless, neglecting to bathe the whole thing in prayer leaves us just workers, not worshippers.

No Excuse Is Good Enough

Prayer is not something we can legislate or make mandatory. It has to flow from each believer's heart to the Lord. It is not my intention to intimidate you into a prayer life or put you on some guilt trip—you must be led by the Holy Spirit.

At the same time, I cannot emphasize to you how

strongly I feel about this. Prayer is such a vital part of our lives as followers of Jesus that nothing is a good enough excuse for keeping us away from it. When we unite in prayer, there is incredible power.

Is prayer mandatory? *It is not.* We cannot create spirituality or put our brothers and sisters under bondage of guilt and legalism.

Is prayer mandatory? *It is!* How can we stay away from it if we are to seriously follow Jesus?

Toward a Richer Prayer Life

If you desire a fresh prayer life and are wondering how and where to start, let me offer a few suggestions that might help you find your way.

1. *Take some time to pray right now.* Humble yourself before the Lord Jesus. Tell Him of your desire to spend more time in His presence. Ask Him to help you know how to pray, and what to pray about.

This is the first major step that you must take before anything else can happen.

2. *As you begin to spend more time in prayer, allow your heart to open up in worship to the Lord.* You see, you need a life of worship on a individual basis, not just during your church's corporate worship time.

What is worship? It literally means to fall down prostrate before the Lord. When you begin to understand who God really is, you will worship Him. Find Bible verses that mention His names and what they mean. Use Scripture to pray—many of the Psalms are beautiful expressions you can use. Sing songs to the Lord. If you don't know any songs, make some up!

3. *Use some common resources to give you items for prayer.* You can easily watch the news on TV or read a newspaper to find out what is going on in the

world. Get ahold of a major newspaper and read the international section. Scribble down some notes about what is happening in Myanmar, Afghanistan, China or whatever countries are mentioned. Begin to pray for the needs of these nations.

Put up a world map in your house. Get a copy of *Operation World* by Patrick Johnstone, which will give you a tremendous amount of information on the spiritual condition of each country in the world. Subscribe to Gospel for Asia's newspaper, *SEND!*, as well as other mission publications. Go through them and make every report a matter of intercession.

Soon you will discover that thirty minutes, an hour or even two hours will not be enough to scratch the surface.

All Can Join the Battle

God in His incredible wisdom has ordained prayer to be the most powerful weapon of the church. If He had chosen anything else—preaching, singing, money or education, for example—many of us could never participate in waging warfare.

But prayer doesn't require any of these things. It can take place anywhere, anytime, and anyone can do it. A housewife, a child, a grandfather, a corporate executive—all are able to impact the world and help change the destiny of millions of lives.

PART V

STRENGTH TO GO ON

Chapter 17

FINDING THE STRENGTH TO STAND

Iplopped myself down in an empty chair in the terminal at Chicago's O'Hare International Airport and heaved a big sigh. I had sixteen days of nonstop traveling and speaking behind me, and now I had two hours between plane connections to catch my breath. Usually I don't mind waiting awhile in the terminal—I enjoy watching people—but that day I grew tired of it.

I was exhausted from sleeping in strange hotel beds with pillows that seemed to grow harder every night. Even the hot chili powder I brought with me to spice up my food had run out. I was emotionally drained from pouring my heart out to groups of people all over the country.

I was feeling sorry for myself. I was angry with the

215

world, with my office staff, with whoever had booked all these speaking engagements for me. I had, of course, approved these meetings, but it felt better to shift the blame away from myself.

I walked over to a pay phone and dialed the Gospel for Asia office in Dallas. I don't even recall who answered the phone, but I distinctly remember saying tersely, "This is K.P. I just want to say one thing: Do not book any meetings, ever again, unless you check with me directly first." I hung up, feeling worse than ever.

I said to myself out loud, "Don't these people understand that I'm not a machine? I'm only a human being." As I wallowed in my self-pity, I knew I had to get up and go on, no matter how I felt. There was a plane to catch in a few minutes. And my life was going to go on. But how was I going to find the strength to continue?

Looking for a Way Out

None of us remains the same in our enthusiasm and commitment. If we are left to our own devices, we will always head the wrong way. The heart of man is naturally wicked, crooked and deceitful. If we do not continually feed upon the things of the Lord—His Word and His presence—we cannot hope to ever finish the race.

You may have begun your walk with the Lord with wholehearted enthusiasm. You were ready to die for the cause of the lost world. But, as time went by, certain things began to eat at that burden on your heart—the distractions and cares of this world, your own personal problems, your friends' enticements, your fears. Suddenly, you find yourself looking for a way to get out of the battle.

You may say to yourself, *Well, when I first made my commitment, the leaders in my church or Bible study really helped me grow. They were on fire for the Lord. But now that I've known them long enough, I can tell they are compromising. It's just not challenging enough anymore. And it's not worth investing my life any longer.* Shifting the blame, just as I did at the airport, is an easy way out.

Know What Is in Your Heart

I have seen this happen in so many organizations and in so many lives! What is actually happening here? Over a period of time you are losing your focus.

God told the children of Israel, "And thou shalt remember all the way which the LORD thy God led thee these forty years in the wilderness, to humble thee, and to prove thee, to know what was in thine heart, whether thou wouldest keep his commandments, or no" (Deut. 8:2).

It seems that God allows adverse circumstances for a reason—whether they be weaknesses, people we work with who rub us the wrong way, decisions we must make that go against our emotions, unfulfilled expectations, misunderstandings, ingratitude, loss of our rights or shattered hopes.

All of a sudden, in the midst of our labors for His kingdom, God takes us and says, "You are in the wilderness. I want to see what will keep you going. When your emotions run dry, when your feelings are gone and there is nothing left to hold onto but bare facts—will you stay with Me?"

Horizontal Motivation

As human beings, we cannot survive any

commitment long without motivation, whether it is godly or self-centered.

Self-centered motivation can be money, power, appreciation—anything that gratifies us. Have you ever wondered why some people go through such incredible pain and agony just to work at a job they hate intensely? They dislike everyone there, and they can't stand what they do. But they stay with it. Do you know why? Because they get a paycheck every week. That is their motivation.

Self-centered motivation can also have a spiritual look to it. We can do wonderful things for the kingdom, and yet we do them because we want to look good, or because we feel guilty if we don't, or because we are emotionally charged from some challenge we heard in the pulpit.

It is terribly easy to fall into the trap of activity. Our motives may be impure, but, *Who knows*? we think to ourselves. There is a danger in the outward appearance of holiness without the inward foundation. This is what A W. Tozer says about horizontal motivation in his book *The Root of the Righteous*:

"The test by which all conduct must finally be judged is motive.

"As water cannot rise higher than its source, so the moral quality in an act can never be higher than the motive that inspires it. For this reason no act that arises from an evil motive can be good, even though some good may appear to come out of it. Every deed done out of anger or spite, for instance, will be found at last to have been done for the enemy and against the Kingdom of God.

"Unfortunately, the nature of religious activity is such that much of it can be carried on for reasons that are not good, such as anger, jealousy, ambition, vanity and avarice. All such activity is essentially evil, and will be counted as such at the judgment.

"In this matter of motive, as in so many other things, the Pharisees afford us clear examples. They remain the world's most dismal religious failures, not because of doctrinal error nor because they were careless or lukewarm, nor because they were outwardly persons of dissolute life. Their whole trouble lay in the quality of their religious motives. They prayed, but they prayed to be heard of men, and thus their motives ruined their prayers and rendered them not only useless, but actually evil. They gave generously to the service of the temple, but they sometimes did it to escape their duty toward their parents, and this was an evil. They judged sin and stood against it when they found it in others, but this they did from self-righteousness and hardness of their heart. So with almost everything they did. Their activities had about them an outward appearance of holiness, and those same activities if carried on out of pure motives, would have been good and praiseworthy. The whole weakness of the Pharisees lay in the quality of their motives.

"That this is not a small matter may be gathered from the fact that those orthodox and proper religionists went on in their blindness till they at last crucified the Lord of glory with no inkling of the gravity of their crime.

"Religious acts done out of low motives are twice evil, evil in themselves and evil because they are done in the name of God. This is equivalent to sinning in the name of the sinless One, lying in the name of the One who cannot lie and hating in the name of the One whose nature is love.

"Christians, and especially very active ones, should take time out frequently to search their souls to be sure of their motives. Many a solo is sung to show off; many a sermon is preached as an exhibition of talent; many a church is founded as a slap at some other church. Even ministry activity may become competitive, and soul-winning may degenerate into a sort of brush-salesman project to satisfy the flesh. Do not forget, the Pharisees were great missionaries, and would compass sea and land to make a convert."[1]

Self-centered, horizontal motivation will not sustain us long. It will only take a few people, our circumstances or our environment to turn us away. We will soon fizzle out in our activity for the kingdom. We can only muster up so much strength from the inside.

We need continuous input. Our physical life is a clear illustration of what happens in the inner man. We must have food and water; otherwise, we will die.

What we need is motivation that is objective— from the Lord.

Out of the Shadow-Lands

As I wallowed in the muck of my self-pity in that airport terminal, I had one of those rare encounters with the Lord. It was as if time stopped for a few moments. I heard a voice in my heart asking me, "Who asked you to do all these things? Didn't I tell you that My yoke is easy and My burden is light? Who made it so hard?"

I realized that spiritually, I was dry inside. I had been so busy in my service for the Lord that I had lost sight of the Lord whom I was serving.

I no longer had what Paul talked about when he said, "I can do all things through Christ which strengtheneth me" (Phil. 4:13). The literal meaning of this verse implies a continual outpouring of Christ's strength. I knew that wasn't the case for me.

"Lord," I said, "I know what You are telling me is true. I am so depressed and tired and weak. But Lord, I want You to help me "

Meanwhile, the ticket counter had opened for passengers to check in and get their boarding passes. I could see the gate behind it beginning to open. Soon I would walk through that doorway and board the plane. As I looked at it, the Lord painted a wonderful picture before my mind's eye.

A few weeks earlier I had finished reading *The Last Battle,* the final book in C.S. Lewis's classic allegorical series *The Chronicles of Narnia.* In them, Lewis tells the story of the adventures of eight English children in the land of Narnia. Aslan, the great lion, portrays a type of Christ throughout the series.

The Last Battle recounts the end of the age for Narnia. As the children watch through a doorway, the old world is completely destroyed before their eyes. Then another land opens up before them. It seems to them almost exactly like the old, yet different somehow.

Digory, one of the older children, explains it to the rest: "...the Narnia you were thinking of...was not the real Narnia. That had a beginning and an end. It was only a shadow or a copy of the real Narnia, which has always been here and always will be here....You need not mourn over Narnia....All of the old Narnia that mattered, all the dear creatures, have been drawn into the real Narnia through the Door. And of course it is different; as different as a real thing is from a shadow or as waking life is from a dream."

Lewis concludes the book by saying, "And for us this is the end of all the stories, and we can most truly say that they all lived happily ever after. But for them it was only the beginning of the real story. All their life in this world and all their adventures in Narnia had only been the cover and title page: now at last they were beginning Chapter One of the Great Story, which no one on earth has read: which goes on forever: in which every chapter is better than the one before."[2]

As I recalled these final scenes from the book, it was time to board my plane.

Then the fog of my self-pity vanished. I could see clearly once again. I realized that all of my aches and pains, my schedule, the bland food, the hard pillows, the strange beds—all of these were just a shadow of what was yet to come. My everyday life here on earth was simply not the real thing. It was temporary and would soon pass.

I looked toward the gate and thought about the door the children had gone through to leave "the Shadow-Lands," as Lewis called them, and enter "the real Narnia."

It was time for me to live again, not for the illusion, but for the reality. I saw that gate to my flight as a door to that reality, if I would choose to accept what was set before me.

I jumped to my feet. I knew I had the strength of the Lord to face the tasks before me. Nothing could stop me now! I marched straight for that boarding gate, through the threshold and onto my next connection.

My heart's attitude was changed. I was no longer running on empty. Once again the strength I was receiving was not my own—it was from the Lord. And the meetings that followed were different somehow. I could tell that, despite the inconveniences, the tiredness and the discomfort, my life was in focus once again.

Search Your Heart

I urge you to examine your own heart. Look at the things you do and the activities you are involved in for the sake of the Lord. Ask yourself honestly, *Why am I doing this?* Search your heart. Be real with yourself.

Jesus told Peter and the disciples, "Pray that ye

enter not into temptation" (Luke 22:40). "Keep thy heart with all diligence," says Proverbs 4:23, "for out of it are the issues of life."

If you are ready to throw in the towel, ask yourself whether you have been depending upon your own self for motivation, or whether the Lord has truly been your source of strength.

During the plagues of Egypt, when utter darkness surrounded the Egyptians, there was light in the camp where God's people lived (see Ex. 10:22-23). Even when you walk through the valley of the shadow of death—the darkest of all darkness—He is still there.

If you are serving the Lord, I am sure you have encountered the same kind of discouragement I faced that day in the airport. In the last two chapters I will talk more about how you can overcome those discouraging times and find your motivation from God.

Living in the Light of Eternity

Chapter 18

ONLY ONE CONCERN

Imagine that you have traveled to Northern India of the early 1900s to a little village, where today a tall, turbaned man is the center of attention. You are now watching a heart-rending scene unfold before you. The man's name is Sadhu Sundar Singh.

As you watch, invisible to the rest of the characters in this drama, the man is about to leave on a long journey. The others, who appear to be his friends, are weeping and begging him not to go.

But you can see from Sadhu's face that although he is touched by their love for him, he is determined to go. He is on his way to Tibet, a forbidding land where evil principalities and powers of Buddhism hold the citizens captive. This is his second or third trip to Tibet. He knows the dangers he faces—and so do his friends and coworkers. They continue to cry out, "Please don't leave us!"

But Sadhu tells them, "I must go to Tibet."

The curtain falls on this scene, and another one begins. Sadhu has arrived in Tibet and is preaching the gospel openly—but he has been seized by the *lamas,* or Buddhist priests. He is a threat to their existence, and they act accordingly.

Sadhu Sundar Singh is flung into the death well, a place no one has ever escaped. He hears the key turning on the face of the well, and he knows that only the head lama has the key. His eyes grow accustomed to the murky darkness. Snakes writhe in the dank hole. Rats skitter around him. There are skulls and bones of those who have been thrown in the well before him.

As Sadhu lies there with a broken arm, in the midst of the filth, he prays this prayer: "Lord, I am so grateful that You have given me this privilege to suffer for Thy name's sake." He repeats this prayer over and over again as the night grows deeper and darker.

Suddenly the well opens, and a rope is thrown down. After a few seconds of utter amazement, Sadhu grasps for the rope and is pulled out of his filthy tomb. When he reaches the top of the well, no one is there....

In the next scene we see Sadhu once again, preaching in the streets of the same village once again. The lamas are totally confounded, for they know that only the head lama has the key to the death well.

Let's allow the curtain to fall on the drama for now and take a closer look at this man's life. It's obvious that Sadhu Sundar Singh underwent times of intense persecution and hardship in his life. Ultimately he laid down his life in Tibet for the sake of the gospel.

Yet, as this real event from his life showed, something allowed him to rise above his circumstances. His strength was not from himself, but from the Lord. This enabled him to endure and rejoice in any and all hardships because he considered it a privilege to serve and to suffer.

Sadhu Sundar Singh had the key to what so many of us are looking for. He knew how to remain constant in his walk with the Lord despite the harsh circumstances he had to endure.

One Thing on His Mind

Read the story of Paul's life in the Bible, and you will find you are reading the story of any normal Christian. Paul was not a superstar or some extra-anointed person. He crafted tents with his hands, making his living like anyone else.

But everything he did—every trip to the market, every voyage in a ship, every tent he made—was insignificant and incidental compared to his real goal in life. He had one thing on his mind: to somehow, some way, pull a few more people out of the fires of hell.

When it came to his own people, the Jews, he said, "For I could wish myself were accursed from Christ for my brethren, my kinsmen according to the flesh" (Rom. 9:3). In simple language, this means he was ready to give his life if it meant his own people would be saved.

What kept Paul going when he was left to die after being stoned? What kept him going when he was shipwrecked? What kept him going when he was misunderstood and forsaken by those around him?

Paul tells us in 2 Corinthians 5:14 that "*the love of Christ constraineth us.*" The Amplified version uses these words: "controls and urges and impels."

Paul was not moved to live the way he lived by any other reason than his relationship with the Lord.

He was motivated to do everything he did for one reason: Jesus. The Lord had spoken regarding Paul when he was first converted: "I will shew him how great things he must suffer *for my name's sake*" (Acts 9:16).

In his letter to the Philippians he wrote, "For to me to live is Christ, and to die is gain" (Phil. 1:21).

Paul could live like this and endure the hardships in his life because of one thing: *He lived constantly for the approval of his Master.*

Hebrews 12:3 says, "For *consider him* that endured such contradiction of sinners against himself, lest ye be wearied and faint in your minds."

Vertical Motivation

Psalm 119 contains some dynamic verses that deal with finding this vertical, objective motivation from the Lord.

Psalm 119:53 reads, "Horror hath taken hold upon me because of the wicked that forsake thy law." Here is a man who is gripped with terrible fear and panic. He is absolutely shaken!

Have you ever seen how a ravenous lion holds his helpless prey by the scruff of the neck? This is how the Psalmist felt—horror had grabbed hold of him.

Why? Did someone beat him up? Did someone violate his rights? Did he lose his salary or have to work overtime? No. *"...because of the wicked that forsake thy law."*

Now let's look at verse 136: "Rivers of waters run down mine eyes, because they keep not thy law." This man is weeping uncontrollably. He cannot stop crying. Rivers of tears are running down his face.

I have cried at certain times in my life. I especially remember when my mother died. I said to myself, *If I don't control myself, I know I will begin to cry. I need to be rational about this. I know she is happy with the Lord and in the best place she can be. I'll see her soon.*

But when I saw others weeping out loud, I completely lost it. I sobbed. I couldn't even stand up any more—I had to hold onto a tree for support. I couldn't handle the thought of my mother's death.

My weeping lasted a few hours, or perhaps a day at the most. This passage says, "Rivers of waters...." This man was brokenhearted. He was weeping nonstop, and why? *"Because they keep not thy law."*

Verse 139 says, "My zeal hath consumed me, because mine enemies have forgotten thy words."

What does it mean when something is consumed? Think about what would happen if you were to pour sulfuric acid on a piece of raw meat. A hiss, a puff of smoke and the meat would be totally gone, consumed by the acid.

This man's zeal consumed him. It had nothing to do with circumstances, problems, treatment from others, failures or loss. No—it was because his enemies *"have forgotten thy words."*

Now let's look at verse 158: "I beheld the transgressors, and was grieved; because they kept not thy word."

In our culture people experience all kinds of hurt in their lives. There are all kinds of reasons for us to grieve, whether it's a personal problem or something imposed upon us. Our own sins may cause it, our expectations may not be met, other people fail us or harsh circumstances may bear down upon us. As a result, we experience sorrow, pain, agony, self-pity, discouragement, disillusionment, mental breakdown and even suicide.

David once said, "Oh that I had wings like a dove! for then would I fly away, and be at rest" (Ps. 55:6).

Do you know what he meant by that? He was wishing for death. Moses felt the same way at one point in his life, when he led the people of Israel out of Egypt—he was ready to quit and die (see Num. 11:11-15).

Yet why was the psalmist grieved in this verse? *"Because they kept not thy word."*

All of his grief had to do with one small word: *thy.*

You Are Mine, Life Is Yours

One of the most beautiful statements I have ever read on this subject was made by E. Stanley Jones in his book *Victory Through Surrender*. He made it a habit to spend time before the Lord, "a time in the early morning when I don't ask for anything but listen to see if God has anything to say to me." And the Lord spoke to him that day:

"He said to me, 'You are Mine, life is yours.' I was startled and asked Him to repeat it. And He did: 'You are Mine, life is yours.'

"That saying has been singing its way through my heart ever since: If I belong to Christ, life belongs to me; I can master it, rescue some good out of everything, good, bad and indifferent....I do not have to be concerned about this, that or the other. I have one concern and only one—that I be His."[1]

If you have any desire to stand firm when trials come, to not be moved by circumstances, to not waver in your faith—you must know this: You cannot even begin to do it in your own strength. You must relinquish your life, and all that it means to you, to Jesus.

I truly believe that this is the kind of motivation that will be required from the people of God if they are to stand firm and even survive in the days to come.

Your only concern is to be His—to be approved by

Him, to please Him, to belong to Him. All that you are and all that you do must be centered around Him and His purposes.

Then, as you walk through this journey called life, every circumstance you face, every emotion you feel—all you experience—will be secondary.

Are you His? Then life is yours.

Chapter 19

RECEIVING A FRESH VISION

The man stopped his hoeing and straightened up, wiping sweat and grime from his forehead. He thought he'd heard unusual sounds coming from the house. Strains of music drifted across the field, and he thought he heard shouts and laughter as well. What was going on?

Well, it was way past quitting time anyway. He heaved the hoe over his shoulder and trudged over the freshly turned-up field toward the house.

As he drew nearer, the music grew louder. He could tell that the wine was flowing freely and the dancing and merriment were in full swing. My father must have real reason for celebration, he thought to himself.

A servant scurried by with a jar of wine. The man called him over. "What is going on here?" he asked.

233

The servant replied, "Your brother has come home! Your father has killed the fatted calf, and we are all rejoicing because your brother is safe and sound. Please, your father wants you to join the celebration—come!"

The man's face darkened. So this was what they were celebrating—his *brother's* return? His irresponsible, wild, loose-living, inheritance-wasting brother? How dare he return after all the years of grief and uncertainty he'd caused? A storehouse of memories flooded back as he thought of his younger brother. Long-suppressed anger welled up and overcame him.

"I will have no part of this celebration!" he spat contemptuously at the servant. "You can tell my father I will not go in!"

The Father's Heart

We are all fairly familiar with the story in Luke 15 of a man and his two sons. We know the younger brother as the prodigal son, but the whole story is really about the father's love.

This chapter begins when Jesus was being criticized by the Pharisees and scribes because He chose to eat with the publicans and sinners. "Look at this man," they whispered to each other. "He says He is God, but look whom He eats with!" They complained about the fact that He was associating Himself with the worst members of society.

Then Jesus told the story of the man and his sons—not necessarily to highlight the prodigal son, but rather to show them the father's heart. He wanted them to understand what God was like.

The Pharisees misunderstood God's holiness to mean that He would not have anything to do with sinners. But Jesus was saying to them, "God has *everything* to do with sinners because He loves them." This story is about the Father.

When we come to the story itself, we see that the younger son represents the sinner, the outcast. The older son is a picture of a believer, someone who knows the Lord and is within the fold.

When the younger son finally returned, what was the older son doing? He was working out in the fields. This man was a hard worker, committed to the father, committed to his fields. In appearance anyway, he loved his father more than his brother did. He never left home, and he didn't gamble his money away.

Jolting the Jar

The older son is a classic illustration of an individual who, in appearance, is doing an extreme amount of good. His life is full of activity. But we soon see that the motivation that kept him going was not genuine love for his father. Therefore, when his brother returned and adverse circumstances bore down upon him, the truth came out. Someone once said, "If you fill a jar with honey, and jolt it as hard as you can, no bitter water will ever come out."

What had happened to the older son? He was perfect—a radical worker. He sacrificed and worked long hours. He faithfully gave money for missions every month. He cut back on his life-style and lived more simply. He prayed an hour every day. He was active in his church. He always went the extra mile.

Am I talking about you and me? Yes, I am.

But as we are in the midst of all this good activity, some adverse circumstances take place.

Wow, we say to ourselves, *I didn't realize I would be rejected so much! I didn't realize I wouldn't get any appreciation for my hard work. I didn't realize this was the kind of requirement I had to live with. I thought there would be more rewards and benefits than this...*

When external pressures bear upon us—and the jar is jolted—whatever is inside comes out. This jolting is orchestrated by the Lord, for He wants us to see what is really in our hearts.

Why did the older son act the way he did? He felt as though he was taken for granted. Something was missing. He no longer had genuine motivation in his heart.

If we look carefully at this passage in Luke 15, we can discover several signs that he had lost this genuine motivation—his love for his father. Let's look at each one carefully.

Legalism

Strangely enough, a person who has lost authentic vertical motivation from the Lord becomes quite *legalistic*. The love of Christ no longer constrains him. He works for the sake of work alone.

If a person is truly motivated by the love of God, he can serve God, work twenty-four hours a day and be the happiest person in the world. He cannot do enough for the Lord because he loves Him so much.

But when you lose that vertical motivation, what happens? Now you are doing things for the Lord because you *have* to.

Legalism also means serving for a reward. The older brother told his father, "These many years do I serve thee ... and yet thou never gavest me a kid, that I might make merry with my friends" (v. 29).

When a person loses genuine motivation and no longer understands what should keep him going, what happens? He sees the Father as cruel. He begins to compare service records. The older brother basically told his father, "I have served you all these years. Look at your other son. He wasted and destroyed everything you gave him."

Do you remember the parable Jesus told about the talents? What did the man who received one talent do with it? He buried it. When he was asked to give an account for it, he told the master, "Lord, I knew that thou art an hard man." (Matt. 25:24). He saw his master as unloving and cruel.

In Matthew 20 Jesus tells the parable of the vineyard owner who hired workers throughout the day to work for him. In the end he gave equal wages to all of them, whether they began at nine in the morning or four in the afternoon.

Do you remember what happened? There was a real uprising from those who started work early in the morning. "Hey," they complained, "this is not fair. We came early this morning. But look at these men! They came late this afternoon, and they received the same wages. You are not doing justice to us!"

"Friend," said the master to one of them, "haven't I given to you what I promised?"

The motivation that kept these men going during the day was something other than what it should have been.

True motivation is love—the oil that keeps the machinery running smoothly. With this motivation, there is no murmuring, complaining or grouchiness.

I like the story about Jacob in Genesis 29. Good old Jacob —what a rude awakening to find out that the woman you married was not the one you expected! And yet we read that all those years of hard labor for Rachel "seemed unto him but a few days," (v. 20) because *he loved her*. He was not working just to feed a few sheep. He was not working for pay. The focus of all his agony was Rachel alone.

Once I spoke to a group of people who were working with a Christian organization on the mission field, and I asked them this question: "If your entire allowance was gone, if your benefits disappeared, if next month you would not earn even a penny—would you still come here? If you had no money even to ride a bus to the office, would you walk here and serve the Lord anyway?"

We must ask ourselves these kinds of questions if we want to avoid the trap of legalism.

Self-pity, Bitterness, Discouragement

The father now pleads with his oldest son, "Please, son, come in with us," but his son refuses. His unyielding, headstrong disposition is a clear indication of a person who is not receiving motivation from the Lord. He refuses to go in because he feels sorry for himself. He is bitter about the whole situation. And he is discouraged.

He has stored his feelings up for quite a long time, and they've been festering until all he can think about is himself. You see, *self-pity, bitterness and discouragement* have everything to do with an inflated ego.

The father is weeping and rejoicing over his younger son. He pleads with his eldest son to come in, but this young man has no feeling for his father or his brother. He can only think of himself.

Jealousy and Love for Honor or Position

A person who is not driven by inner spiritual motivation from the Lord will experience *jealousy* over others' blessings. He will be driven to *desire honor and position*. This could be manifested in desiring to be noticed by others, looking for opportunities to tell others what he has done, never wanting to take second place or secretly expecting appreciation or approval from men.

When our heart is not motivated by love, our relationships with others are strained.

The older brother had no problem until his younger brother came home. He was happy and content. He probably never would have complained at all if his brother hadn't come home. He would have stayed in the field, day after day, faithfully working.

But when his brother came home, he thought, *All the attention I get, all the benefits I receive, all of my father's love will now be turned to him. Now that this brother of mine has returned, look at the embracing, the ring, the shoes, the new clothes. Look at the feast, the dancing and the celebration!* The older brother was jealous of all the attention his brother was getting.

Before Paul became a believer, his main desire was to eliminate Christianity. Now, if you were a believer during that time, you would have a hard time accepting this new convert, wouldn't you? "It's just a ploy," you might say. "He is only coming to find out who we are, and then he'll kill us." This is exactly what happened. No one trusted Paul (see Acts 9:26).

Then Barnabas came along and put his life on the line for Paul. He vouched for him and convinced others that Paul truly had been saved. A wonderful partnership was begun.

A few chapters later in Acts, we no longer read about "Barnabas and Paul." Now we read "Paul and Barnabas." Fascinating! Barnabas willingly took second place to Paul. You see, his motivation was not based on honor or position. Barnabas simply loved Jesus, and he wanted to serve Him.

It is the sign of true godliness to desire nothing but

the Lord Himself. It is not a simple thing to take second place and let someone else get the honor. It can only be done by someone who understands and follows the heart of God.

Pride

The older brother told his father, "All these years—*I* have done your work." Notice also that he didn't say "my brother" but "your son." He was filled with *pride,* with an exalted opinion of himself.

He didn't even have room in his heart to acknowledge this tramp standing there, weeping and repenting, as his brother. There was no room in his life for weak people.

When we work as a team, as a church, as a fellowship, we must remember this: the body of Christ is not made up of all superhuman entities. The body of Christ is made up of some weak, broken-legged, half-blind, bruised, hurting children. The body of Christ is filled with weak, failing, sinning and repenting people. It seems to me from this story that God has more compassion for them than for the superstars.

This older son didn't understand his father's heart. Remember, this story is about the father and his all-embracing, all-forgiving, all-encompassing love. But this son was not touched by that love, even though he was living in the same house and working for him. He didn't understand. A weak, failing, backsliding man stood before him, and all the elder brother could say was, "Well, it was coming to him."

True motivation from the Lord will manifest itself in humility. Instead, we see an "I'm better than you" attitude. There is no concession for weak, failing people.

Because the older brother was not in touch with

the love of his father, he compared others with himself. His estimation of himself was quite high—it was pride.

Lack of Love for Others

We do not read in this story that the older son went out to look for his brother when he was gone. All this man could think of were the horrible things his brother had done. Who told him his brother was living with prostitutes and doing wicked things? How did he find that out? Obviously there was no confession from his younger brother. But read what the older son tells his father: "this thy son ... hath devoured thy living with harlots" (Luke 15:30). *There was no love in his heart*—he expected the worst from his brother.

Jonah went to Nineveh and preached a fiery sermon, warning the Ninevites that they would soon be destroyed for their wickedness. The whole city repented, and God's anger was turned away. He decided not to destroy them.

In Jonah 4 we find Jonah very angry with God because of His decision.

"Why are you angry, Jonah?" God asks. "Is it right for you to be so angry?" And Jonah fumes, "Of course! I have every reason to be angry!"

"Jonah," He says, "there are thousands of people here who do not know their left hand from their right. They are blind, they are dying. I have compassion on them. Don't you? Can't you feel what I feel?"

Jonah replied, "I knew that if I went and preached to these people, they would repent; and You are a merciful and compassionate God, and You would forgive them." What a strange rationalization! Jonah knew his theology well, but it was only head knowledge. He didn't understand the Father's heart.

The story of Ruth is a fantastic drama. In the first

chapter Naomi tells her daughters-in-law, Ruth and Orpah, "Look, my children, this is it. There is nothing I can do for you. Your husbands are both dead, and I have no more sons for you to marry. Go home and get married."

I think Naomi was smart. I wonder if she was testing those girls to see their responses.

What did Orpah do? She decided to go back home.

The Bible tells us, "But Ruth clave unto her." She told Naomi, "Intreat me not to leave thee, or to return from following after thee: for whither thou goest, I will go; and where thou lodgest, I will lodge: thy people shall be my people, and thy God my God" (Ruth 1:14,16).

Going with Naomi meant that Ruth would be leaving all that was ever familiar to her—her family, her culture, even the gods she worshiped. She was leaving it all behind her.

How could Ruth make such a decision? Because she loved Naomi. *Love made it possible for her to leave everything.*

When you lack love for your brothers and sisters around you, it is a clear indication that you are not motivated by the love of the Father. When you become short-tempered and impatient, rejecting others and expecting the worst from them, remember this: No good can come out of this, even in the work of the Lord.

Wanting to Give Up

The sixth sign of erosion in genuine motivation is *desiring simply to quit.*

The older son now speaks to the father, "I have done all these things for you, and you haven't done a thing for me! Seems like a one-way street to me. I am on the short end of the stick all the time. I am the one who has to give, and give, and give. I am the one who is suffering. You have given nothing to me—there is no relationship here at all."

In 2 Timothy 4:10 Paul tells Timothy that Demas basically packed up his bags and left him. All of us, at some point in our lives, will face the temptation to quit. Some will be tempted to give up their Christian life entirely.

"I can do all things through Christ which strengtheneth me," says Paul (Phil. 4:13). If anyone ever had a reason to quit, Paul did. But he tells us, "No, I won't give up." There was something beyond what he could see or tangibly deal with that motivated him.

Unwillingness to Suffer

Inconveniences, trials, difficulties and living with less will cause many people to lose their motivation. This is because *we often forget to include suffering in love*.

The elder son lacked something that his father had—a tender heart toward his brother. Any feelings of love that he might have ever had were buried deep beneath his resentment, bitterness and anger.

His father, however, wasn't afraid to love his youngest son, even if it meant suffering terrible hurt over the poor choices he had made in the past.

No love is genuine love unless there is suffering in it. C.S. Lewis talks about the risks of true love in his book *The Four Loves*:

"To love at all is to be vulnerable. Love anything, and your heart will certainly be wrung and possibly be broken. If you want to make sure of keeping it intact, you must give your heart to no one, not even to an animal. Wrap it carefully round with hobbies and little luxuries; avoid all entanglements; lock it up safe in the casket or coffin of your selfishness. But in that casket—safe, dark, motionless, airless—it will change. It will not be broken; it will become unbreakable, impenetrable, irredeemable.

"The alternative to tragedy, or at least to the risk of tragedy, is damnation. The only place outside Heaven where you can be perfectly safe from all the dangers and perturbations of love is Hell."[1]

Jesus' motivation was His pure love for His Father. In obedience He came as a man and shared His Father's heart for the lost world. And the love that was in His heart included suffering. If it had not, we still would not have a Redeemer.

Lack of Prayer

Although it is not specifically mentioned in the story, I seriously doubt that the older son had any real heart-to-heart communication with his father. He certainly did not share his father's heart of compassion; I don't even think he understood it.

If we are not motivated to do what we do by the love of God, we will surely dry up in our prayer life.

A church or an organization that is not motivated by the living God and His Word will rely upon agencies, plans, programs, schedules and all sorts of gimmicks to get the job done. What will keep us going in the feast and the famine will be the type of relationship with the Lord that only prayer can bring.

Unwillingness to Live by Faith

The father told his older son, "All that you see around you—look! It is yours! It has always been yours. Now or later—you are mine, and all that I have is yours. I love you, and I care about your younger brother too. It is all the same."

But the son *could not live by faith.* He couldn't understand what his father was telling him.

Paul told Timothy, "the time of my departure is at hand.... there is laid up for me a crown of righteousness, which the Lord, the righteous judge, shall give me at that day..."(2 Tim. 4:6,8). Paul looked forward to that day in faith.

We read in Hebrews 11 of a group of people who lived, suffered and died in faith. Faith motivated them. Even though they did not experience the promises of the Lord in their generation, they looked toward the day when the promises would be fulfilled.

When your faith and trust in the Lord are lacking, you know you are not being motivated by that vertical, objective motivation from Him. You are not looking directly to Him as your source, and suddenly the circumstances look pretty grim. You become weak inside because His strength is not flowing through you.

Only a Shadow Remains

Have you lost this vital, vertical motivation? Do you see yourself in the pages you've just read?

Self-motivated persons can be very active in the service of the Lord. But they can also be very demanding and judgmental.

Even when someone loses his or her first love for the Lord, he or she can still be vigorously involved in the work of the Lord, expressing intense concern about the moral condition of society or becoming zealous for world evangelism. However, the internal relationship is gone—only a shadow of that reality remains. But a person can still appear as committed as ever.

In 2 Samuel 12, when Nathan approached David after David had sinned with Bathsheba, Nathan told him a story about two men. One was a rich, greedy, perverse man who owned hundreds of sheep; the other was a poor and honest man who owned only one little lamb.

When David heard that the rich man had taken the only lamb of his poor neighbor and slaughtered it to feed a visitor, he was enraged. "Who is the rat?" he thundered to Nathan. "He deserves to die!"

Then Nathan told David, "You are that man."

David was so overzealous about the condition of his people that he failed to see that he was the real culprit.

Paul talked about a group of people who were sold out for preaching the gospel, but for the wrong reason. Their intent was to cause more persecution for Paul, who was in prison at the time for preaching the gospel (see Phil. 1:15-16).

It is so easy to try to live the Christian life on our own. Now that we realize what has gone wrong, how do we go about mending it?

Repent

In Revelation 2 we read Jesus' message to the church in Ephesus. It's an incredible passage that can turn your stomach upside down!

If you remember the story of the Ephesians from Acts 19, you will know that when Paul preached the gospel to them, a great number believed. They brought their sorcery books, which were worth fifty thousand pieces of silver, and burned them publicly. They took a stand against darkness and were totally committed to Christ, separating themselves completely from their former ways of living.

The Ephesians were enlightened with the greatest of truth (see Eph. 1:18); they were blessed with every spiritual blessing (see Eph. 1:3).

But read now what Jesus tells them: "I know thy works, and thy labour, and thy patience, and how thou canst not bear them which are evil: and thou hast tried them which say they are apostles, and are not, and hast found them liars: and hast borne, and hast patience, and for my name's sake hast laboured, and hast not fainted. Nevertheless I have somewhat against thee, because thou hast left thy first love. Remember therefore from whence thou art fallen, and repent, and do the first works; or else I will come unto thee quickly, and remove thy candlestick out of his place, except thou repent" (Rev. 2:2-5).

There is a fascinating paradox in this passage: Jesus first tells the church some incredibly positive things. "I know your work, your labor and your commitment," He says. But then He tells them, *"Repent, and do the first work."*

There we find the paradox. First He says, "You are doing all these good things." Then He tells them, "Repent, and do the same things."

Perhaps the Lord would say something similar to a believer today: "You are giving ten thousand dollars every month to My work, but I am going to snuff out your light unless you repent."

"Lord," the believer says, "what do you want me to do?"

"Repent," says Jesus, "and give ten thousand dollars a month to My work."

At first it sounds confusing, doesn't it?

But do you see what Jesus says is missing in these people's lives? "Thou hast left thy first love."

Before, the Ephesians had been motivated by love. First Thessalonians 1:3 talks about the "labour of love."

Now the Ephesians worked and labored just the same as always, but their inner motivation had changed. Now all that they did was for themselves, not for the Lord.

When you discover yourself in a situation like this, the Lord wants you to come to Him and say, "Lord, I am doing all these things, but now it is only mechanical. The spring is wound, and things keep going and going, but my heart no longer feels the same burden. I don't have the same love for the lost. I do these things because I have to do them. It has been a long time, Lord, since I cried over the lost world. My concerns have turned to myself—my own sorrows and my own problems. Please, Lord, give me that real, genuine heart motivation once again."

This is true repentance. It is not patching up old wineskins, but becoming new wineskins, fresh once again. I encourage you to take that first step of repentance.

Surrender

I thank God for that day over twenty years ago when a group of Operation Mobilization workers, myself included, gathered in an old school building in North India. George Verwer spoke to us from Hebrews 4, and his message was this: *"There remains a rest for God's people. Enter into it."*

I will never forget that day. It was the day I surrendered myself completely to the Lord. I was one of the people who went forward and said, "I am fighting, struggling and striving, I am always hurting and in pain; I am always complaining that something is wrong. I want rest."

I realized that day the incredible reality of entering into God's rest. Once you surrender your life completely to the Lord, no matter what happens from then on, you have something to fall back on. It is all in God's hands, and you can say, "Lord, it's all Yours."

Be Filled with the Holy Spirit

There is no more important factor in living a victorious life—one that is filled with motivation and strength that come from beyond ourselves—than *being filled with the Holy Spirit.*

Many people are confused about what it means to be filled with the Holy Spirit. I am not going to dictate to you about the "how" of being filled with the Spirit of God—it doesn't matter so much to me how it happens. Just make sure that you *are!*

The Word of God tells us we are walking into very dangerous times in history when many will fall away. Remember, God wiped out a whole generation and saved only Noah and his family. The majority will not make it. God is looking for a small minority who are living holy lives and are willing to walk in His footsteps.

We must not be persuaded by the trends of this world. We must make sure that we are led by the Spirit of God.

As Unto the Lord

What is the key to living with right motivation? *Do everything "as to the Lord, and not unto men"* (Col. 3:23). This is a statement we hear often, but the real meaning comes when you interpret it practically.

It is said that if you do anything for twenty-one days, you will have established a habit. For the next twenty-one days, no matter what you are asked or called to do, say to yourself, *I am doing it for the Lord.... I am doing it for the Lord.*

Watch how this becomes part of your thinking—and part of your life!

Think About Heaven

Why should we *think about heaven?* If a person works at a job, what does he look for? His paycheck.

The "paycheck" is what Paul says he is looking for when he writes, "there is laid up for me a crown of righteousness" (2 Tim. 4:8). Isaiah prophesies, "Behold, the Lord GOD will come with strong hand, and his arm shall rule for him: behold, his reward is with him" (Is. 40:10).

Read through the book of Daniel and look at his life. This man was pulled out of his homeland, put in prison then given a job and misunderstood. His life was one of giving and serving, giving and serving. He had no wife or children. His life was completely devoted to serving others.

He was thrown into the lion's den. But he kept on serving. Kings came and went, kingdoms changed hands. Daniel became an old man.

Toward the end of the book an angel appeared to Daniel and told him, "Daniel, it is your time to rest. Don't worry about anything. You will be given your reward."

Why, in the last few moments of this old man's life, did God come to him and tell him these words? I don't know the exact answer, but I suspect that Daniel, in the midst of all the ups and downs in his life, had something on his mind. *Someday*, he may have said to himself, *this is all going to be over. This is not final. This is only a short time that I have to walk through.* When the angel spoke to him, it was an affirmation of his convictions. "You have done well," the angel told him.

In the final hours of his life, Paul said to Timothy, "I am going with the knowledge that the Lord has reserved a crown for me." That knowledge kept him going. He was able to say confidently, "For our light affliction, which is but for a moment, worketh for us a far more exceeding and eternal weight of glory" (2 Cor. 4:17).

Think about heaven. In everything you have to live with and deal with each day, think, *This is not the end. There is more, and this is only a short time that I will be walking through.*

The Lord has promised us through His Word that the end will be better than the beginning. Don't lose heart. Let's take Him at His Word!

PART VI

LIVING IN THE LIGHT OF ETERNITY

Conclusion

A PRAYER

Lord Jesus, we want to thank You for Your grace and mercy that forgive and cleanse us, that pick us up and motivate us to continue on our journey with You.

Lord, we realize that we are not living in a neutral zone. We are living in the enemy's territory. The Bible tells us that the whole world lies in the lap of the wicked one. O Lord, we are so aware that the god of this world is our enemy.

We know that the more we seek to please You, the more we seek to do Your will, the more we pray, the more we reach out to the lost world, the more we accept the cross, the more we will be faced with the fiery darts of the evil one.

And, Lord, it seems so often that the battleground is in our minds. How often—even daily—we face discouragements, questions, doubts, concerns, agonies, misunderstandings and self-pity. How often we find ourselves wanting to get out of the battle, to run off and hide somewhere. How often we find our hearts getting cold. It is all part of this struggle we are in. We are soldiers who sometimes get wounded and hurt. We have to lie low when the bullets come straight toward us.

Yet, Lord, we know that whether we stand or fall, we are still in Your hands. Today we surrender our lives to You once again completely; we want You to take absolute control of our hearts.

Thank You, Lord. Thank You for encouraging us and motivating us. Thank You for Your love that fills our hearts. Thank You for giving us every weapon that we need to continue in this warfare. Thank You for encouraging us and giving us peace. Thank You for filling our hearts with joy and giving us strength. In Jesus' precious name, Amen.

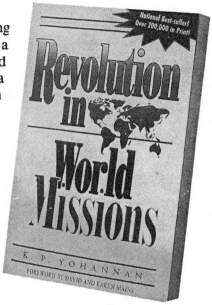

You Can Be Part of Reaching Millions for Christ!

Yes! I care about the lost and forgotten millions of Asia. I am interested in learning more about the ministry of Gospel for Asia and the native missionary movement.

In the USA or Canada call
1-800-WIN-ASIA (946-2742)
for more information on the ministry of Gospel for Asia and a FREE one-year subscription to
SEND!—**The Voice of Native Missions.**

For mail orders complete the form below.

❖ ❖ ❖ ❖ ❖ ❖ ❖ ❖ ❖

☐ **Please send more information** about the ministry of Gospel for Asia, including a FREE one-year subscription to *SEND!*—**The Voice of Native Missions.**

Name _____

Address _____

City _____

State/Province _____ Zip/Postal Code _____

Telephone ( ) _____

Total enclosed: $_____

Please mail to:
Gospel for Asia

USA - 1932 Walnut Plaza, Carrollton, TX 75006
Canada - P.O. Box 4000, Waterdown, ONT L0R 2H0

Notes

Chapter 6
1. Amy Carmichael, *Thy Brother's Blood Crieth*, (Dohnavur Fellowship, originally published by Morgan and Scott).

Chapter 9
1. C.S. Lewis, *The Screwtape Letters*, (New York: Bantam Books, 1982), p. 39.
2. A.W. Tozer, *The Root of the Righteous*, (Harrisburg, PA: Christian Publications, 1955), p. 52.

Chapter 10
1. E. Stanley Jones, *Victory Through Surrender*,

(Tiruvalla, Kerala, India: Gospel for Asia Publications, 1991), pp. 17-24.

Chapter 11
1. Juan Carlos Ortiz, *Call to Discipleship*, (Plainfield, NJ: Logos International, 1975), pp. 42-43.

Chapter 17
1. A.W. Tozer, *The Root of the Righteous*, (Harrisburg, PA: Christian Publications, 1955), pp. 89-91.
2. C.S. Lewis, *The Last Battle*, (New York: Collier Books, Macmillan Publishing Co., 1970), pp. 169-170, 184.

Chapter 18
1. E. Stanley Jones, *Victory Through Surrender*, (Tiruvalla, Kerala, India: Gospel for Asia Publications, 1991), p. 42.

Chapter 19
1. C.S. Lewis, *The Four Loves*, (New York: Harcourt Brace Jovanovich, 1960), p. 169.